CAMBRIDGE LIBRARY COLLECTION

Books of enduring scholarly value

Philosophy

This series contains both philosophical texts and critical essays about philosophy, concentrating especially on works originally published in the eighteenth and nineteenth centuries. It covers a broad range of topics including ethics, logic, metaphysics, aesthetics, utilitarianism, positivism, scientific method and political thought. It also includes biographies and accounts of the history of philosophy, as well as collections of papers by leading figures. In addition to this series, primary texts by ancient philosophers, and works with particular relevance to philosophy of science, politics or theology, may be found elsewhere in the Cambridge Library Collection.

Psychology of the Moral Self

After more than ten years teaching ancient Greek history and philosophy at University College, Oxford, the British philosopher and political theorist Bernard Bosanquet (1848–1923) resigned from his post to spend more time writing. He was particularly interested in contemporary social theory, including the social ramifications of the growing field of psychology, and this book, published in 1897, is a collection of his lectures on this topic. The ten lectures explore many aspects of psychology and its relationship to larger philosophical and ethical issues. Bosanquet poses the question whether psychology takes a subjective point of view, while other sciences take an objective one. He discusses classic psychological themes such as the ego, the soul, self-consciousness, emotion and feeling, and individual volition. Bosanquet's observations in these concise essays offer the perspective of a leading nineteenth-century thinker on this growing and influential field of scientific and social inquiry.

T0341995

Cambridge University Press has long been a pioneer in the reissuing of out-of-print titles from its own backlist, producing digital reprints of books that are still sought after by scholars and students but could not be reprinted economically using traditional technology. The Cambridge Library Collection extends this activity to a wider range of books which are still of importance to researchers and professionals, either for the source material they contain, or as landmarks in the history of their academic discipline.

Drawing from the world-renowned collections in the Cambridge University Library, and guided by the advice of experts in each subject area, Cambridge University Press is using state-of-the-art scanning machines in its own Printing House to capture the content of each book selected for inclusion. The files are processed to give a consistently clear, crisp image, and the books finished to the high quality standard for which the Press is recognised around the world. The latest print-on-demand technology ensures that the books will remain available indefinitely, and that orders for single or multiple copies can quickly be supplied.

The Cambridge Library Collection will bring back to life books of enduring scholarly value (including out-of-copyright works originally issued by other publishers) across a wide range of disciplines in the humanities and social sciences and in science and technology.

Psychology of the Moral Self

BERNARD BOSANQUET

CAMBRIDGE
UNIVERSITY PRESS

CAMBRIDGE UNIVERSITY PRESS

Cambridge, New York, Melbourne, Madrid, Cape Town,
Singapore, São Paolo, Delhi, Tokyo, Mexico City

Published in the United States of America by Cambridge University Press, New York

www.cambridge.org
Information on this title: www.cambridge.org/9781108040846

This edition first published 1897
This digitally printed version 2012

ISBN 978-1-108-04084-6 Paperback

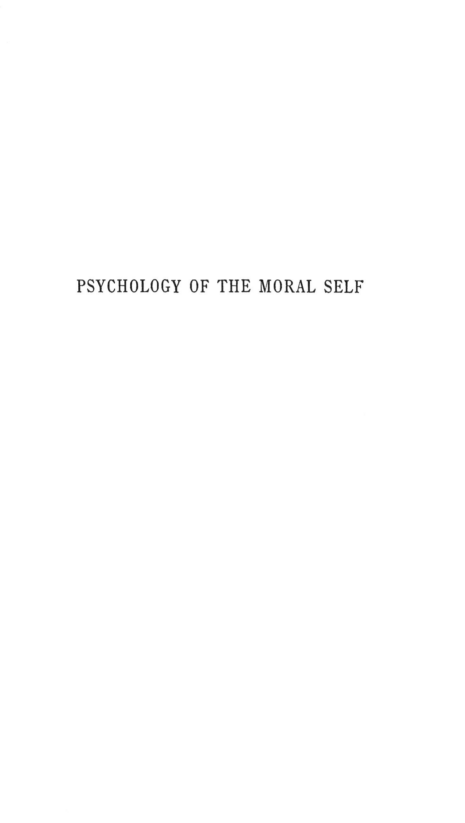

PSYCHOLOGY OF THE MORAL SELF

PSYCHOLOGY

OF

THE MORAL SELF

BY

B. BOSANQUET

London
MACMILLAN AND CO., Limited
NEW YORK: THE MACMILLAN COMPANY
1897

PREFACE

IT seems clear that a work is needed which should treat of modern psychological conceptions in their bearing upon ethical problems. No doubt, psychology is still full of controversy, and fundamental questions are *sub judice*. But it would be an exaggeration to assert that no dominant tendency is now discernible in the best psychological thought. The doctrine of Apperception, and such an idea as that of "vital series," which is implied though not insisted on in the present work, are far enough advanced to throw a wholly new light upon the nature of Will, considered as the man in relation to action. When I say "a new light," I mean a light which is new as compared with the popular philosophy of the last generation. For that the most recent psychology is definitely corroborating the notions of Hellenic as of modern idealism, constitutes its absorbing interest, and its claim on the ethical student. Besides Mr. F. H. Bradley, my debt to whom need not be further insisted on, I have found the groundwork of my psychological ideas in the writings of Professor William James, Mr. Stout, and

Münsterberg. Professor Sully's *Human Mind* has also been of great service to me, and constitutes, if I may venture to express an opinion, a striking advance upon his earlier writings.

My principal acknowledgments are due, however, to my wife, whose assistance in reducing my lecture-notes to readable form renders her share in the work about equal to my own.

I am aware that these lectures are brief, and even curt. But I believe that they will give a useful clue to students who desire to approach moral philosophy with some genuine ideas on the nature and working of mind.

I have added at the end of the book a bibliographical note, for beginners, and the questions which were set week by week to the students attending the lectures. They serve to insist upon the main points of importance.

B. BOSANQUET.

LONDON, *March* 1897.

CONTENTS

LECTURE I

LECTURE II

LECTURE III

LECTURE IV

LECTURE V

LECTURE VI

LECTURE VII

LECTURE VIII

LECTURE IX

LECTURE X

LECTURE I

THE PSYCHOLOGICAL POINT OF VIEW

1. IN explaining the subject with which we are dealing we may begin by contrasting such a term as the "province" of a science with its "point of view." Botany, for instance, has a "province," or a denotation; that is, a distinguishable class of material objects with which alone it deals,—there is no botany of rocks or gases, but only of plants. Botany, indeed, has a "point of view" as well as a province, as we see when we compare it with medicine, which deals with plants in so far as they have a specific action on the body; the point of view is a different one. But it remains true that the "point of view" of the science is limited by its "province," and *vice versâ*, in much the same way as in logic we say that connotation is limited by denotation. Every natural science is thus restricted to a certain range of objects

In Psychology the case is different. The limit is one of "point of view" only, and no special province can be marked off. Some writers (*e.g.* Mr. Sully in *The Human Mind*) attempt to limit the science by saying that it deals with internal as opposed to external experience; but as Mr. Ward points out

(*Ency. Brit.*, Ninth ed., vol. xx. p. 37), the distinction is either inaccurate or inapplicable.   It is generally used as meaning " in the mind " opposed to " in space," with a more or less vague implication that the contents of the mind are ideas, and similar impalpable entities, while the contents of space are solid things ; but the antithesis is an unmeaning one, owing to the ambiguity of the word " in " in its double application to consciousness and space.   The conception of being " in " space is a familiar one ; what is meant by being " in " a mind or " in " consciousness we shall consider directly.   Sometimes the distinction is merely used to indicate what takes place within the limits of the body as opposed to what takes place without those limits ; but in this sense it does not distinguish the province of Psychology from what falls outside Psychology, since Psychology deals with all perceptions whether of internal or external events.

In the same way the distinction between "mental" and " material " fails to help us in marking off our province (see Mr. Ward, *l.c.* p. 38), unless we explain it as a mere difference in the point of view we take. Unless, that is, we say that a material object when considered as presented in experience is mental, and so belongs to Psychology, and when not considered as presented does not.

Thus we find that we must come to a distinction by the point of view from which Psychology works, and not by the province with which it deals.   Then the question arises—Can we say that Pyschology takes a subjective point of view, and all other sciences an objective one ?   Here again we must answer in the negative.   If we are distinguishing, say, logically

or ethically between our presentations, then some of
them will be more subjective, and others more objective ; but for Psychology there is no such distinction.
Nor is the science specially *uncertain* because it deals
with *mental* facts ; as objects of observation and
inference they are just as good as any other facts,
and as a science Psychology must take itself to be
objective, *i.e.* to be such as any rational being would
construct with the same data. This suggests the
distinction which has been made by Mr. Herbert
Spencer, and adopted by Höffding (translation, p. 24),
between Subjective and Objective Psychology. According to this distinction, Objective Psychology
includes " physiological and sociological data," while
Subjective Psychology deals with the " natures of
particular modes of consciousness, as ascertained by
introspection." But, if we regard them from the
point of view of throwing light on mind, all our
facts, whether we borrow them from physiology and
sociology, or whether we glean them from introspection, are equally objective. It is only when
they are considered for their value from a philosophical point of view that the former constitute *par
excellence* objective mind.

Mr. Ward himself (*l.c.*) suggests as a distinction
that Psychology takes an individualistic point of
view, while other sciences take one that is universal-
istic. This seems to mean that the psychologist
deals solely with facts of presentation to *particular
minds*, while the student of natural science neglects
this characteristic, and thinks of his objects quite
apart from their relation to particular minds. If we
accept this we must be careful that it does not tie
us down to any assumption about the individual

mind being there to begin with, or remaining limited
to any particular source of self-feeling or content, as,
e.g., the body.   We must leave ourselves quite free
to study the growth of mind in its earlier stages,
and all possible sources from which it may derive
its content.

Keeping in mind the necessity of this freedom
we may try two other definitions.   James, in his
Text-book of Psychology, adopts one given by Ladd :
"Psychology is the description and explanation of
states of consciousness as such."   Here we are met
by the difficulty that consciousness is as yet a
disputed term, that there is no agreement among
psychologists as to what facts are included in it, or
whether or not it covers the whole of psychical or
mental life.

The second definition is one given by Bradley
(*Mind*, O.S., xii. 354).   Psychology "has to do
with psychical occurrences and their laws," *i.e.* with
the facts experienced within a single soul, considered
merely as events which happen.   "Experience" and
"soul" are here used as very wide terms, which do
not commit us at starting to any assumptions about
consciousness or self-consciousness, or about the
"subject" and similar conceptions.   Experience
cannot be defined in any way, for it is all inclusive,
and leaves nothing by which it can be limited ; we
can only, as it were, point it out, or indicate it.

2. Psychical events, then, or the facts experienced
within a soul, together with their laws or ways of
happening, form the subject-matter of Psychology.
What do we mean by "*in* a soul?"   Bearing in
mind what we have said about the *point of view*, we

may reply, "everything that goes to make up its world." Here we have to recall the distinction made in introducing the lectures on logic (*Essentials of Logic*, p. 7); the distinction between the psychological and logical modes of regarding the contents of the mind. The formed world—*e.g.* as it exists for me in space, or, again, *your* mind to me—is *more than* an event in my mind ; but it *is* an event in my mind, and it is only from this latter point of view that Psychology considers it. What *more* it may be is a question for other sciences. To use an illustration, we may say that the psychologist is merely a looker-on, an observer ; and that to him your mind, with its contents or object, is like a microscope with its object to one who looks at it from the outside. *You* are interested in the object for its own sake, but he does not want to know about this primarily ; he is interested in finding out by what machinery it was focussed and illuminated, what caused it to be thus before you, and what will cause it to disappear again and bring something else in its place. *In this sense* there is no object in your world which is not in your soul, and Psychology only considers it *as* in your soul.

The sciences, indeed, which deal with the organised reality, although clearly differentiated from Psychology, may themselves afford material for psychological treatment. Æsthetics, *e.g.*, treats of mental contents from the point of view of their capacity for yielding æsthetic pleasure or emotion, and the mind that is trained to æsthetic enjoyment may afford very different material for psychological study from the mind that is not so trained.

Logic, again, has an entirely different sphere from

Psychology in that it deals with mental events as material for the construction of reality; and its principles are not psychological laws, but principles by which reality is constructed. But all the same, a mind which is swayed by a logical principle, whether consciously or unconsciously, will differ psychologically from one which is not, or from itself when not under the influence of the principle; the mental contents will be differently organised in the two cases, and will thus afford different material for the psychologist.

3. It will help us here if we mention, merely in general, what Aristotle had to say about the nature of the soul. It will show, that is, how the problem presented itself to a great man approaching it while it was comparatively fresh and free from preconceptions about immortality, free-will, and ·muscular contraction. We may notice :—

(a.) It presents itself to him as a matter of gradation. It is difficult to say where the soul begins; there is vegetative mind or life, sensitive mind, rational and volitional mind. In proportion as the order of Nature takes on a certain individual and apparently purposive form, the problem of mind begins and it continues upwards into consciousness. Here we can see no apparent dread of materialism, or at any rate of continuity with the unconscious; and it is very hard to find out what was thought by Plato and Aristotle of the relation of the Soul to consciousness. They think more of order and the appearance of purpose than of mere consciousness.

(β.) The definition is more like that of a problem

or a postulate than of a thing. Mind, he tells us,
begins with " The simplest mode of self-realisation
of an organic body." This leaves room for other
modes of mind above, and growing out of, the
simplest, and does not tie us down to any mode of
subject or substance; we might paraphrase it by
saying that "mind is the way in which the unity
of an organic body displays itself." He afterwards
distinguishes to the best of his power the different
phases of the psychical, as we also must endeavour
to do, and in so doing he connects infant Psychology
with that of animals.

The point is, that stating the problem in this
large way enables us to approach it quite differently
from the way in which a ready-made dogmatiser
approaches it. We are led to look at the mind,
prima facie, as beginning a long way down, and as
a sort of struggle towards unity. I do not say
that this view could be true, *e.g.*, in metaphysics;
but it is very convenient to be allowed to take it
in Psychology. We grant readily that we cannot
explain mind as a co-operation of bodily parts—of
monads or the like; nevertheless, it does seem to
be a co-operation of elements in experience, elements
which are not merely drawn from our own body,
but which all ultimately appear to have definite
connections in the environment which we construct.

4. The soul, then, for us is simply our immediate
experience, which we take as belonging to a thing
that has past and future, in a way just analogous to
that in which we construct anything in space and
give it identity. We trace our soul backward, and
construct it from our given experience. The word

"immediate" perhaps needs explanation here; it is used to exclude the real world which is the content of experience. If this was included, as we saw, the soul would be everything. But though the soul *is* not in the full sense everything which it knows, yet it is *different* because of what it knows; the content, or world of realities, of course affects the immediate experience, giving it colour and definite filling.

5. The abstract ego is a different conception from that of the soul, and we need not really trouble ourselves with it in Psychology. It represents the argument that the subject which knows must be other than the object which is known, and that it must be identical throughout. As to the *prima facie* truth of this we may note what actually takes place in our ordinary conceptions of the self, which seem to involve a constant transposition of content between the self and not-self. (See Ward, *Ency. Brit.*, Ninth ed., vol. xx. p. 39). At one time the self is identified with the body, and at another it is distinguished from it, while there is always a tendency to describe certain phases or regions of consciousness as the real or true self, as opposed to others with which we are less inclined to identify ourselves. But the point is that the self, in Psychology, seems always to be identified with some positive content, and not always with the same. Whether or not there is a positive identical nucleus of presentation is still a question for discussion. But what we would suggest is that the abstract ego is merely a way of describing one characteristic of the concrete self, and does not really help to explain it. At all events, it could be of no use to us in Psychology

unless it declared itself in some way by affecting
the sequence and connections of our presentations,
and this seems only possible through some positive
content ; a mere abstract point would not impose
any special direction or grouping upon our presentations. And if it merely represents the general
character of these presentations themselves—their
tendency, for instance, to reproduce one another in
certain ways—we want only this character itself in
so far as it works, and need not trouble ourselves
with any theory about its origin.

Conclusion.—This, then, is the picture of a soul
which I have tried to suggest ; not a ready-made
machine working on certain material, but a growth
of material more like a process of crystallisation,
the material moulding itself according to its own
affinities and cohesions. The nervous system may
indeed be regarded from one point of view as
a pre-existing machine ; but not psychically, for
it constitutes no special part of our presentations. Given this view we may ask, looking at
the general purpose of our lectures, " Ought a
spiritual philosophy to be content with such a view
as this ? " This, of course, is only an objection
which *might* be urged, not one which should be, for
Philosophy has no right to dictate to Psychology.
But our answer would be " Yes ; it is just a *spiritual*
philosophy which *can* be content with it." If you
think the whole universe is mechanical or brute
matter, then we can understand your trying to keep
a little mystic shrine within the individual soul,
which may be sacred from intrusion and different
from everything else—a monad without windows.
But if you are accustomed to take the whole as

spiritual, and to find that the more you look at it as a whole the more spiritual it is, then you do not need to play these little tricks in order to get a last refuge for freedom by shutting out the universe.

It has always been the most spiritual philosophy that has been most audacious in simply taking the soul as an operation or appearance within the universe, incapable of being cut off from other operations and appearances, and demanding to be investigated quite impartially with reference to the origin and connection of its elements. There is nothing to be afraid of in finding that the operative content, the actual being of the soul, comes from the environment. How else, indeed, should we have a real communion with other souls?

LECTURE II

1. BEFORE going on to consider the general nature of psychical events it will be well to say a word about the attitude we should take in interpreting what different psychologists may have said. In all such interpretations there are two pitfalls to avoid. In the first place we must be careful not to force every difference of expression between one writer and another into a difference of principle. For instance, Locke's use of the term idea for any presentation is probably peculiar to himself, but when we understand the sense in which he applied it we find that it covers no difference of principle. On the other hand, we must not allow ourselves to deny that there are differences of principle, on the ground that the different terms employed must have referred to experience which is the same for those who use them. The only safe rule in critical history is to study our writers as a whole, and see what they really wished to maintain; what the whole drift of their language supports. There is, of course, such a thing as confusion of thought; where the writer himself has not been clear as to what was involved in his statements. We may perhaps find an instance

of this in Mill's theory of inference from particulars to particulars.

2. The history of modern Psychology may be said to begin with Hobbes, and is at first mainly concerned with the doctrine of Association. (See Croom Robertson's article in the *Encyclopaedia Britannica* on " Association "). This doctrine was taken up by Locke and Hume, but is said to have been first thoroughly applied to the whole of mind by Hartley. For our present purpose we may consider it as it developed in the hands of Locke and Hume.

They were the authors of the " Psychological Philosophy " which has so frequently been criticised. The necessary effect of narrowing down all Philosophy into Psychology is to cut away the material of Psychology itself. The method employed is to begin by laying it down that the validity of ideas depends upon their mode of origin, and not upon self-evidence ; and then to proceed by inquiring into this mode of origin in the history of the individual mind. Thus the problem which presents itself to them is that of putting together the mind and the world out of mere psychical events, out of irreducible facts or data. By refusing to take more than what is given, they are tied down to the consideration of events in the soul, and this leads to subjective idealism, because all ideas may be regarded as events in the soul, and any question as to what validity they have as making up a world belongs to a different enquiry altogether. Moreover the followers of this method are prevented even from stating the full nature of the events in question ; for these events have an aspect which affects their nature as events, although it is not their nature as events, and is therefore disregarded by the psychological philosopher.

When, therefore, he begins the study of this mental history, the psychological philosopher is first struck by those fairly discriminated presentations which occupy the focus of attention in the mature intelligence. He sets to work to classify these as Locke does ; and he classifies them under the most obvious heads of distinct sources of sensation (especially the five senses), and obvious modes of reflection. Locke,[1] indeed, is aware that sensations are altered by the judgment, but he does not press this idea so far as to recognise the close interconnection of all mental elements. On the whole it seems fair to say that he, and still more Hume, takes as a type of the mind the very brightest centre of the focus of attention, disregarding all the mass of presentations which, as we are now taught, make up the soul. But the focus, of course, may change very sharply. If, *e.g.*, we take our memory of the leading presentations during a whole day, without forcing or cross-questioning ourselves, it may be like a string of beads without any apparent connection—cabs, streets, persons, work, eating, the newspaper—a mere set of lantern slides ; indeed, *as we remember them* they will not even be dissolving views.

Now this was naturally how Locke and Hume tended to look at the train of ideas. From their point of view there was nothing to be gained by more subtle and complete investigation. Their

---

[1] *Essay*, Bk. ii. ch. ix. sect. 8.

interest was to know, in the first place, whether our
more important ideas either of sound and colour or
of space, or again of substance and causation or of
the self, were irreducible data ; and, secondly, how
they came to cohere or to be associated together.
They rummaged about in experience and found
what they looked for—the most striking events in
the soul ; and having found them they were soon,
and rightly, satisfied that the history of the individual
soul is a history of events, which, as events, as
irreducible data, gave no purchase for stepping
across to anything from them.   Nor would a deeper
investigation, if conducted from the same standpoint,
have directly influenced their views ; although indirectly it would have done so, and in the long
run it did greatly help to alter the views of their
successors.   For Hume, then, the mind was like a
string of beads without the string, or a peal of bells,
and this is what we mean when we speak of
Atomism.   (Atomism is merely the Greek form for
individualism, only it happens that atom has come
to mean a thing and individual a person).   There
appear to be two stages of Atomism ; the first, in
which it is a sheer fiction and is now a thing of the
past, the second, in which it involves a psychological
confusion which we must consider more in detail.

(i.) As a statement of Hume's theory of simple
sensations and ideas as units of the mind we may
quote the following passage (pp. 320, 321, Black's
edition, vol. i.).

" It is evident that the identity which we attribute
to the human mind, however perfect we may imagine
it to be, is not able to run the several perceptions
into one and make them lose their characters of

distinction and difference, which are essential to them.   It is still true that every distinct perception which enters into the composition of the mind is a distinct existence, and is different and distinguishable and separable from every other perception, either contemporary or successive."

And again, " What we call mind is nothing but a heap or collection of different perceptions united together by certain relations, and supposed, though falsely, to be endowed with a perfect simplicity and identity."

This kind of description is a sheer fiction if it implies that discriminated sensations and ideas are a primitive constant and the only contents of the mind.   Probably this is what it did, on the whole, imply in Locke, making due allowance for the passage above quoted,[1] where he says that sensations are modified by the judgment.   Really this passage only serves to emphasise the doctrine, which we can trace henceforward in all the British psychologists down to Bain inclusive.

To bring out what is implied in the doctrine, take as an instance the sort of vision an artist has of clearly discriminated colour patches ; these are sensations perhaps most nearly approximating to Hume's distinct perceptions.   Can we think that a baby, near the commencement of its psychological experience, has anything like these clearly defined sensations ; or must we not rather regard them as the result of a long process of education in discrimination ?   What is really meant by the single sensation which we find alluded to in psychological manuals ?   Is it a primary and fixed constituent

[1] *Essay*, Bk. ii. ch. ix. sect. 8.

in all perception; or is it, as experienced by an adult, a result of discrimination which normally disappears in perception? In other words, is mental growth a process of compounding units distinctly given, or is it rather a process of discrimination within a mass which cannot and does not change its character all at once (as the focus of attention may do from moment to moment) because it is not all attended to in the same measure at once.

It is important for the student to note carefully the line taken by psychological text-books about this. To note, that is, whether they represent mind as compounded out of given units by a process of association, or as growing by differentiation of a continuous tissue or texture. It is interesting in this respect to compare Sully's earlier and later books (*Outlines of Psychology* and *The Human Mind*), and to note also how far the structure of his book tells the same tale with its doctrines. James, in the preface to his text-book, explains that he prefers to proceed " from the more concrete mental aspects with which we are best acquainted to the so-called elements which we naturally come to know later by way of abstraction. The opposite order of ' building up ' the mind out of its ' units of composition ' has the merit of expository elegance, and gives a neatly subdivided table of contents ; but it often purchases these advantages at the cost of reality and truth . . . we really gain a more living understanding of the mind by keeping our attention as long as possible upon our entire conscious states as they are concretely given to us, than by the *post-mortem* study of their comminuted ' elements.' This last is the study of artificial abstractions, not of natural things."

Ward's account of the psychical continuum (*Ency. Brit.*, Ninth ed., vol. xx. p. 45) is quite clear, and should be carefully read. "We are led," he tells us, "alike by particular facts and general considerations to the conception of a *totum objectivum* or objective continuum which is gradually differentiated, thereby becoming what we call distinct presentations, just as with mental growth some particular presentation, clear as a whole, as Leibnitz would say, becomes a complex of distinguishable parts. Of the very beginning of this continuum we can say nothing : absolute beginnings are beyond the pale of science. Actual presentation consists in this continuum being differentiated, and every differentiation constitutes a new presentation." The Atomism which denies a psychical continuum in this sense is a fallacy very like (and contemporary with) the fallacy of the social contract in its crudest form ; it antedates the independent existence of the individual.

We have said that, indirectly, better observation on psychological ground has done much to rectify this fallacy. We may mention two points with reference to which this is specially noticeable : (*a*) less conscious or sub-conscious presentations; (*b*) one special portion of these—organic sensations.

(*a*) With regard to sub-conscious presentations in general, it was probably Herbart who first drew attention to them. By employing the conception of the "threshold of consciousness," and thinking of presentations as rising above or falling below this threshold according as they are more or less clearly present, we avoid the mistake of confining our theoretical considerations to that part of consciousness which we are most definitely attending to. We

C

may illustrate this from the focus of vision. When we fix our eyes upon any object so that it is clearly discriminated—that forms, as it were, the centre of our vision, but does not cover the whole field—there is much that is not attended to, that is out of focus, and therefore indistinct. In the same way the presentations which occupy the focus of attention at any moment are really the smallest part of what the mind has present to it; there is a field which is occupied by presentations which are not in focus, and therefore not discriminated, and the whole state of consciousness takes its colouring very much from these. This sub-conscious mass changes very slowly, and in every person probably has certain permanent and many habitual elements, and in this way goes far to bind consciousness together as one whole. It is interesting to connect this theory of sub-consciousness with the question of *Feeling* and the elements of thought and reason which are implicit in it, and which enable it to serve as a real principle. (See Hegel, *Hist. of Philos.* (E. Tr.), iii. 400.)

(*b*) The so-called organic sensations consist of all the obscure sensations that go to make up our bodily comfort or discomfort; the total result is sometimes called the Cœnesthesis or "common feeling." This does not seem to be noticed by Locke or Hume, but it is noticed in Bain. It forms a very important factor in the psychical continuum, for though it is not usually in the focus of attention, it is always in the margin, and forms the background of our whole conscious life. While it persists, our sense of our identity remains unshaken, whatever vicissitudes we may undergo; while to grave changes in it are probably due such pathological phenomena as the "duplication of the ego," or the hallucination of poisoning which is apt to accompany the onset of lunacy.

To omit these elements as absolute facts of psychological observation was sheer omission of psychical material on the part of the older psychologists. By taking this material in, our view of the mind is made much more concrete. The simile of a series, or collection, or train of ideas now yields to that of *mass* and *wave* (the base of the wave containing the marginal, its crest the focal elements), of which all the parts react on each other.

(ii.) But even when we have accepted the psychical continuum and the psychical mass or wave, there is still the question as to how we should regard its continuity. After all is said, it remains true that each pulse of mind, each advance of the wave, in one sense each presentation, *is* an event which never recurs. We need, therefore, some account of the nature of the continuity or identity of this continuum ; and it is quite possible for the essential faults of Atomism to continue along with the recognition of a mass or wave of presentations as a psychical fact. We may, that is, continue to confuse the *events* with their *reference* or meaning.

A very fair test as to whether psychologists make this confusion is their statement of the Law of Association (here we are anticipating). *What* is it that Association marries ? events in the soul or generalised contents ? Take Bain's statement (*Mental or Moral Science*, p. 85)—" Actions, Sensations, and States of Feeling, occurring together in close succession, tend to grow together or cohere in such a way that when any one of them is afterwards presented to the mind, the others are apt to be brought up in idea." Clearly what we have here is a resurrection of mere events. (For a further criticism of this view see Ward, *Ency. Brit.*, Ninth ed., vol. xx. p. 60.)

A further test of the presence of this confusion is the use of the "Law of Obliviscence" as a normal part of the Associative process. If A suggests *d*, it is said, it does so because it suggests *a*, which was formerly presented as *abcd*, and so is connected with *d*; but because only *d* is now suggested, it is necessary to account for the disappearance of *abc* by the law of obliviscence, by the action of which they are so attenuated as to become invisible links. In other words, on this theory, in order to get from the A which suggests to the *d* which is suggested, we must, it is said, go round through the details of a former presentation. But since these details do not appear in consciousness, it is obvious that we cannot verify them, and the question is whether we really go through them at all. I pass a particular house, and it recalls to me a friend who used to live there. Must I on principle, suppose that my mind has gone round—unconsciously—through the details of some former event in which he and the house were con-nected—say a call which I made there on the 2nd of May ; or may I not suppose simply that a general connection has been formed by which one part of the content directly reinstates the other? As an instance of the misleading influence of this theory, we may notice its application (first by a clergyman named Gay, and afterwards by Hartley and others) to the problem of means and ends. The miser, it is said, begins by desiring money—like other people—for what it will get ; it is at first only a means to other ends. By what process does he come to make the money the one end of his existence to the exclusion of all others? The Associationists explain that it is because the feelings formerly connected with the ends have become gradually associated with the means so closely that finally they become transferred to it. (See Bradley's *Ethical Studies*, p. 60.)

With this ordinary law of Association we may now compare Bradley's statement (*Mind*, O.S., xii. 358). " Every mental element when present tends to reinstate those elements with which it has been presented." An " element" here means any distinguishable aspect of the matter or content, and not any particular *event* in the soul. We need not here go further into this question, which has been raised in this lecture merely to explain Atomism. But we must bear in mind that we shall always have Atomism *in principle*, until the content of the soul connects *itself together*, and in order to do this it must go beyond events to meanings. So long as the work of connection is thrown upon " attention," or " the subject," and so long as events are connected instead of contents, we continue to have psychological confusion.

What is really wanted to complete the idea of the psychical continuum is a true account of identity. This must just reverse Hume's doctrine (*l.c.*) that identity is added to the string of perceptions by the observer, who thus comes to regard the mind as identical with itself. Identity must *really belong* to the perceptions, and unite them together. The question is, whether we take identity to consist in the exclusion of difference; if we do, we have Atomism, and can get no further than A is A. We shall return to this later.

LECTURE III

COGNITION—THE GROWTH OF CONSCIOUSNESS

IN this lecture we have to consider what Cognition is from the point of view of Psychology; in other words, we have to consider the development of a world as it takes place *de facto*. The question of the *validity* of the cognition does not primarily concern us. In our next lecture we shall consider more in detail the processes by which Cognition develops.

Our criticism of the doctrine of Association may be supplemented by contrasting the term itself with such terms as "community," "corporation," or "unity." It implies that the view taken is of independent units, which are the same in the combination as out of it, and are tied or linked as such by Association; and historically it really originated in such a view. The general truth implied in it is, that phases of the soul, such as presentations, can be traced in time, and that a sort of causation, or at least a natural sequence, can be observed in them; the real principle being, however, not a linking of units, but organisation by identities of content.

Our starting-point, then, must be different from that assumed by the doctrine of Association strictly taken. It must be a continuous presentation, to be described either as feeling, or, as others would say, as having the three aspects of feeling, conation, and sensation (or cognition). The conception is that of a direct experience which *is* a multiplicity of determinations, but does not distinguish them ; a state prior to consciousness, and also continuing as one side of consciousness. The question is important as an attempt to get something which embraces our whole psychosis as a single experience—as ourself. Then, if we call it Feeling, it is not feeling in the sense of *mere* Pleasure or Pain. But there is not a very great practical difference between the two views, for there must *be* movement and variety in feeling, and it becomes merely a question of how we ought to describe their presence in a very simple state of soul. For instance, there would be change in feeling as the presentations changed, but not at first a feeling of succession ; that needs some one (or more) group of presentations which is felt as persistent against the rest. Thus movement would *be* there, but how would it be presented ? We have to imagine a more or less vaguely felt continuum, gradually differentiating itself into qualitatively distinct sensations, and then developing into the consciousness which is so varied as to have the appearance of being made up of many different elements and aspects. In its earlier stages this vague continuum might be like our dream-world, through which ghosts of presentations are constantly gliding without any attempt on our part to organise them, or mould them into the solidity of reality. Hence the saying that there is no surprise in dreams ; every wave of presentation just *is*, and we accept it without speculation as to its source or reason.

The problem for Psychology is to get from this vague continuum, or dream-world, to our waking world, as organised in Space and Time, and as contrasted with our mere ideas—the world to which, in our Cognition, Perception is especially relative.

We are capable of Perception in the most general sense when we have erected a persistent group within our presentations into a " real object," *i.e.* into something which is a presentation, but is more than a mere presentation, and which therefore exercises constraint on the course of psychical events. Objects in space are the simplest instance. With them there arises the distinction between signs and objects ; *mere* ideas are signs.

In order to get to this stage from the mere mass of feeling which *is* the undeveloped soul, the chief matter of principle is to obtain the distinction between changes in the presentation mass which are due to its previous course, and changes which maintain themselves against its course, or which seem to interfere with it, to collide with or guide it. This is the germ of the distinction between mere idea and reality, and it is only with reality that we get to Cognition. To work out the development would involve an account of a very long stage of evolution ; but there is no doubt that the force at work is that of interference—as a rule, of disappointment.

In order to account for the development we have to assume—

(i.) That the total presentation has recurring elements.

(ii.) That a presented element tends to reproduce

the elements with which it has been presented (a
form of the laws of Association) in such a way
that there is a tendency to form groups.

(iii.) That there are movements in the organism
which are brought about by, and themselves bring
about, changes in the presentation mass, and that
these changes are pleasant or painful.

Then the general type of process would be:
change in the presentation mass, say an indication
of food within reach, followed by a movement which
is felt, and is such as has previously brought about
another change in the presentation mass, say contact
with the food. If the movement always succeeded
in bringing about this second change, it is difficult
to see how progress should take place. But if we
suppose the movement (which is felt) to fail, then
it would result in two contradictory presentations
tied together. The change in the presentation would
be forced to analyse itself, to break up into conflicting elements. The movement would in part
produce the same feeling as before by its effect on
the outside of the organism (we leave out for the
present *motor* feelings, if there are any), and this
would *re*produce by association the feeling of contact
with food and consequent pleasure; but the fact of
failure would actually *produce* a different feeling,
possibly contact with some substance that caused
pain. The two elements would struggle, there would
be tension and pain, and finally the objective one,
as we call it—the one corresponding to the physical
fact—would drive the other, or *merely* mental element,
out.

At first this is all nothing more than a succession
of psychical modifications. Strictly speaking, we

cannot say that it is expectation and disappointment, because the suggestion of contact with food
simply came as a fact of presentation, and we must
not assume that at first the soul treats it as an
expectation—*i.e.* as something which promised or referred to a future fact of a different order from itself.

But *after* experience of the conflict then the
suggestion of pleasure would tend to become a *mere*
expectation ; that is to say, when the feeling of the
movement was *again* suggested it would bring the
collision of feelings along with it ; the suggestion of
the food would be there, but accompanied by a
suggestion of possible failure, and this must ultimately lead to the required distinction when, after
the movement, the presentation either occurs or
does not occur.

The conflict would then give rise to a distinction
between the continuous psychical course and the
grouped and recurring presentations that have power
to constrain or disappoint it.   The conflicting *suggestions* of pleasant and painful contact necessarily
come to be distinguished from the unambiguous
presentations which the reality will give ; and finally,
a psychical suggestion would come to be regarded as
a mere separable sign of the constraining presentation,
—a sign, that is, which might be experienced apart
from the presentation, but is no longer a single fact
in its own right.

Perception would then become possible.   Its
essence would *not* be the mere blending of a
psychical suggestion with a presentation having
points of identity with it—not merely a feeling of
food *reinforced by* contact with real food and so
maintaining itself ; it would be the blending of ideal

elements by identity with the objective presentation *after* the two have passed through a thorough opposition to each other, and the sign is distinguished from the thing signified. THIS is what I wanted, or THIS is my food. F is *f.* Then at last the blending through identity of points in the content means a judgment.

Perception of Space (Inner and Outer).—Our explanation of the Perception of Space, and of how it has been developed, will depend again upon whether we accept or reject psychological Atomism. To the Associationist, Space can be constructed by the linking together of sensations which originally formed one or more Time series, and then by occurring simultaneously became associated into the perception of Space. This, however, really amounts to saying that sense of Space is at bottom the sense of Time ; and that is quite contrary to the facts of experience. (See Ward, *Ency. Brit.*, Ninth ed., vol. xx. p. 53.)

On the other hand we make the problem even harder than it is by treating elementary presentations as if they had to be either inward or outward in the developed sense. This is a distinction which only appears later ; for we cannot have *Inner* except in contrast with *Outer*. Thus the problem is not in any case one of changing inner presentations—*i.e.* mental changes, *known as such*—into outer ones ; but of differentiating a given world, a world which would not present itself as changes in a mind, as a *time-series*, but simply as a given mass.

Ward and James express this non-inwardness which precedes the development of full spatial character, by saying that "extensity," as the mere possibility of differentiation, is primitive. James, indeed, seems to say that *all* sensations are extended in three dimensions—*i.e.* that they all contain the element of voluminousness, which is the original sensation of space; a view which seems incomprehensible, *e.g.*, about sound. Nor does it seem likely that his belief in an original third dimension of space, which is perceived *immediately*, can be justified. But there is no doubt that, whether we accept the term "extensity" or not, sensations of touch and sight must have from the beginning a kind of *more and less* which is other than *in*tensity; that is, they must have spatial character, parts outside one another, and capable of being recognised as outside one another in the developed consciousness.

When we have assumed spatial quality as belonging to certain of our presented groups, then recognisable feelings of movement and contact help us to give definition to the size and relative position of those groups. All localisation must have its origin in reference to the body, and the first question which arises is the question as to how sensations are localised by the subject in different parts of the body. The process can only be explained by assuming some difference in the sensations themselves, or their accompaniments, which enables us after experience to assign them to some definite position in space. The sensation must contain or be accompanied by some *sign* indicating the locality at which the stimulus is felt. One suggestion has been that every nerve conveys in addition to the sensation an "extra-impression," which serves as this local sign, and indicates to what position the stimulus which gives rise to the sensation is to be referred. Lotze, in discussing the nature of this extra-impression, suggests that no stimulus, not even the prick of a pin, is really confined in its effect to a mathematical point, but that owing to the continuity of the skin there are accompanying displacements, each in its turn giving rise to its special subordinate sensation which accompanies the main sensation in consciousness. This would fulfil the requirement " that all the spatial relations of the stimulus acting on us should be replaced by " (or translated into) " a system of graduated qualitative tokens," or local signs. (Lotze, *Metaphysics*, Bk. iii. ch. iv.; see also Ward, *Ency. Brit.*, Ninth ed., vol. xx. p. 54).[1] When we have succeeded in developing this system of local signs—when, that is, experience has enabled us to differentiate them out of the original vague continuum—then we are able to refer things to their places in connection with our bodies.

Another question arises as to the perception of distance. Is it only obtained by association with touch and movement, or is it a true optical sensation? James seems to maintain that it is seen immediately, and is not merely constructed from our experience. But strictly speaking it is not visible; in the line of vision point covers point, and it is only as plane surfaces emerge that there is anything to be seen. It is our interpretation of the relations between these plane surfaces, as given in their sizes and colouring, and combined with our experience of movements, which enables us to construct a third dimension, *i.e.* to see distance. But James's conception of measurement by *things* which we identify seems very true as an account of the development of the perception.

[1] For a criticism of Lotze's view, see Külpe's *Outlines of Psychology* (E. Tr.), sect. 61.

Touch and movement are necessary to give us the first idea of the third dimension, but the presentational groups would help to develop it. Here we see how much depends on the identification of presentational groups. Spatial reality *is* the system of groups which we connect with our bodies.

So also in Time; the essence of the perception depends on the formation within the psychical continuum of groups that have phases. But in order that *succession* may give rise to the *idea of succession*, there must be something which is recognised as interesting and *persistent* throughout the successive phases. It seems natural to suppose that the interest in succession (such as expectation, or the contrast of the *actual* present and the *unreal* future, and memory as introducing expectation) would exist long before what we mean by Time arose—that is, before any idea of *comparative* duration arose. Tenses have been said to arise out of moods.

Probably at first, Time would be merely a system of occasions or signals for action, which would thus be much like any instinctive action, and it might have very little to do with sense of duration. Birds will go to roost in an eclipse, accepting the darkness as a signal, without regard to the time at which it occurs, *i.e.* to the duration of the day. But this naturally develops into a process of holding together the phases of *two* groups, which may of course be one's bodily feelings and another group, and noting how far they coincide. *Failure* to coincide would be especially noticeable; "mid-day sun and no food!" and the fear that the light would go before food was obtained would give rise to interest in succession. James's idea of measurement by things perhaps applies in Time also. It seems doubtful whether we begin measurement by *accurate* phases of the body group; though we might begin with hunger. The phases of those objects which demand customary action would develop the idea of comparative duration by the attention directed upon them. If we take for instance the distinction between winter and summer nights, the difference of length could suggest itself very slowly. An animal might by instinct avoid a long chase on a winter's day, and try it on a summer's day; but when a creature came to remember and notice that it could go very much further by daylight in summer than in winter, then we have the germ of a comparison of duration.

The essential for any idea of succession at all is, that several phases of some rhythm should be held together in memory against some constant element; and this is the germ of comparing two sets of phases together by asking how many of the one rhythm go to one of the other? It is impossible to compare directly the phases of the *same* succession. *There is no attempt at accurate judgment until we come to simple physical theory*, such as is involved in the water-clock or the sand-glass; there is, indeed, no *need* to ask whether the days are *equal*, so long as sunrise, noon, and sunset adequately dictate our movements.

With regard to our construction of the temporal series, Ward suggests that it is effected, or at least facilitated by the "movements of attention." The adjustments of expectation, etc., may be remembered, and so help us to throw a series into order when we look back upon it; but unless there were also some *reason* for the order the tendency would probably not be very strong.   The judging of *short* intervals, again, has to do with the rhythm of respiration, etc., but this is not the principal source of division used for practical purposes.   That is always axiomatic, resting on the assumed constancy of some natural process, as in the examples above referred to.   (Cf. author's *Knowledge and Reality*, p. 329).

Physical Reality implies both Space and Time ; Space as relation to the body group, and Time as the idea of persistence apart from our psychical course.   It has been shown above how we endow things with separate existence in order to explain contradictions, due to change of phases contradicting the suggestions of our psychical course.

Consciousness. — Consciousness as opposed to unconsciousness is taken to cover all soul-life ; but in this sense it must not be identified with consciousness *par excellence*—the state of mind which definitely has an object before it, and seems to have little or no content for the subject ; the state of mind, that is, which regards the objective world as a given something which is not itself.   This is the position of common sense, and it is continued by abstraction in the physical sciences, which, as we saw, take no notice of *being in the soul* at all, but treat the process of knowledge as a mere analysis of something given outside the self.   No doubt consciousness may be bound to become *self*-consciousness as soon as we reflect upon it, but the position of common-sense is that it does not reflect.

Is not the body the self in early soul-life ?   Not exactly so ; there is more *and* less in the nucleus of the Self from the first ; and the body is gradually passed over into the objective world.   This process

really leads up to a reaction.   Common-sense ends
by passing everything over into the "other," *e.g.*
when we discover that sensation is not at the nerve-
tips, we begin to treat nerves as outside mind ; but
this "other" is being organised, and really is the
organised content of the soul ; although we, in our
common-sense stage, have forgotten that it is so,
and have set it over against the bare abstract Self,
thus preparing for another stage.

LECTURE IV

THE ORGANISATION OF INTELLIGENCE

1. THE central point of our last lecture was the development of cognition as it takes place in the formation of groups within the psychical continuum. In this lecture we shall consider the names given to different aspects of the processes by which these groups are formed and react upon one another in such a way as to develop thought. We shall find that these processes fall under two main heads, Blending and Reproduction. The aspects known as Assimilation, Discrimination, and Apperception belong chiefly to Blending ; while Association belongs to Reproduction. (The subject of *attention* is too wide to be dealt with here. It may be regarded either as a general name for the laws according to which presentation takes place, or in a more special sense for volition.)

2. Assimilation and Discrimination are generally treated as correlative processes, both employed in the " elaboration of mind " (see Sully, *Human Mind*, chap. vii.), but of an opposite tendency. The fact is, that apart from the theory of identity (see Lecture II.), their relation is very hard to state. Generally

speaking, they are regarded as alternating, first a little of one and then a little of the other; and according as psychologists have a preference for one or the other, that one is represented as being of primary importance, and preceding the other. (See Sully, *l.c.*) We seem to get nearer the truth if we regard them both as different aspects of one and the same process. Certainly we can hardly describe the one without implying the other.

(*a*) Assimilation is *elementary recognition* (see Ward, *Ency. Brit.*, Ninth ed., vol. xx.), the mere *perceiving* as like; that is to say, it is recognition unaccompanied by any process of localisation, or of conscious comparison. In this sense it is recognition in its earlier stages, or the germ of recognition.[1] The process is something like this: a change in the presentation continuum such as has taken place before, recurs; in recurring, it coalesces with the residuum of its former occurrence, and it thus appears as familiar; *i.e.* it is recognised as a previous experience, even though the circumstances of its former occurrence cannot be reproduced.

Why does the recurrence of a change make it seem familiar? The mere reinforcement by the residuum of a previous change may make the impression stronger or clearer than it would otherwise have been, but there seems to be no reason why it should give rise to a feeling of familiarity, the *consciousness* that it has been there before. This

---

[1] I do not feel sure whether the note of familiarity, of " I have seen that before," which marks assimilation *par excellence*, is present in all perception in an appreciable degree, except where there is distinct unfamiliarity. In returning to one's own house or room it is certainly there. But the interest of a positive perception—the "what is it?"—often dwarfs the "seen before."

must probably be due to a *suggestion* of *difference*. The change itself has occurred before, but under different circumstances, and therefore with different psychical accompaniments. As the new content blends with the residuum of the old, two different contexts, the present and the past, are brought together, and we are aware—more or less consciously—of the same content in different settings. This is what constitutes familiarity. The process is thus a twofold one ; the blending of new and old brings to light, or at any rate suggests, difference, and at the same time the element of identity is reinforced. For instance, I am looking for a street, but have forgotten its name. Suddenly I come upon it and recognise it ; *i.e.* in the first place I *notice* the name ; I pick it out from amongst all the others because it is emphasised by blending with the subconscious residuum. But this by itself is not enough. I might notice it because it was written in larger letters, and so emphasised above the others ; and mere noticing is not recognition. But as I notice the name it also faintly suggests the past context in which it was presented, and which differed in some respects from the present ; thus a difference, a vague vista of continuity reaching beyond the given context, is suggested, and the feeling of familiarity appears ; the feeling of, as it were, comparing the presentation with itself and finding it the same.

Strictly speaking, to assimilate would more naturally mean to *make* like, than to recognise as being like. Wundt brings this out clearly by insisting on the way in which we are apt to transfer the different context of our present perception to the previous one to which it is assimilated, or *vice versa*, of the previous perception to the present one. This may be done to a degree which actually amounts to illusion ; our preconceived idea actually modifies the presentation as we receive it. He gives as an instance the illusion produced by the rough daubs of the scene-painter, which are supplemented by, or assimilated to, our former experience of land-scapes, and so endowed with the qualities of reality. It is, no doubt, a question how far there is an illusion by means of the transference of differences, and how far the presentation does actually undergo change.

Why do the groups of presentations within the psychical continuum form as they do ? Why, that is, do not colours group with colours, smells with smells, and touches with touches ; instead of feel and colour and smell combining together in one group as one thing ? One reason, no doubt, is that Association does not take place—as it has so often been said to do—by similarity. (See Ward, *Ency. Brit.*, Ninth ed., vol. xx., p. 56.)

But the chief reason is, that the groups, in the first place, are *given* in this way, and in the second, *act* (*i.e.* are interesting for us) in these combinations. Sensations of the same sense, such as two colours or two sounds, tend to exclude each other. It is sensations of different senses that can most naturally be presented together, and when the group has been formed the one sensation becomes a sign of the others. Groups which constantly cohere in this way come to be assimilated (recognised) as wholes which affect us, and are therefore discriminated from the background because of their importance for life, before their elements are *separately* assimilated and recognised as qualities. In science, that is when we

begin to reflect upon them, we do arrange our sensations in qualitative series ; we disengage them, that
is, from the groups in which they are originally
given, and re-group them according to their kind.

(β) This leads us to *Discrimination*. Here we
may note some points in James's chapter on Discrimination (*Text-book*, p. 244). In the first place
the elements to be discriminated must, as he says, *be*
different if we are to know them as different. But
difference does not of itself make discrimination.
Two different elements may be presented without
the difference being noticed ; this corresponds to an
unassimilated presentation. As James points out,
impressions, to be discriminated, must be *experienced
separately* by the mind. But here we must be careful to define what we mean by *separately ;* an isolated
impression is never experienced. The point is, that
any element, before it can be discriminated, must be
presented in different surroundings or in a different
context. Further, the elements to be discriminated
must have a common basis. Take as an instance
" goodness " and " two o'clock." Each is itself, the
two are quite different, but there is neither assimilation nor discrimination between them ; there is no
psychical relation at all. We cannot have discrimination, *i.e.* felt or perceived difference, without a
fight on the basis of identity, without having the
same content in different contexts (see last lecture),
and this begins with assimilation. The very sense
of familiarity has the germ of difference in it, of
persistence through two contexts.

Using a formula, we may say, A is given in two
contexts, AB and AC ; when it is presented again
it suggests both B and C, which must conflict until

they find a *modus vivendi*.   This *modus vivendi* is a relation of difference.   " When a red ivory ball, seen for the first time, has been withdrawn, it will leave a mental representation of itself, in which all that it simultaneously gave us will indistinguishably co-exist. Let a white ball succeed to it ; now, and not before, will an attribute detach itself, and the *colour*, by force of contrast, be shaken out into the foreground.   Let the white ball be replaced by an egg, and this new difference will bring the *form* into notice from its previous slumber, and thus, that which began by being simply an object cut out from the surrounding scene becomes for us first a *red* object, then a *red round* object, and so on " (Martineau in James, *l.c.*). Or we may take as another instance a tree as it appears with its leaves off, and again with its leaves on ; here what is needed to make us recognise it as the *same* tree under different conditions is the relation of time-difference, with all that it involves.   But quite at first no definite relation is perceived ; there is simply a feeling of familiarity, of persistence ; a feeling, that is, of a former context accompanying assimilation.

3. *Apperception.*—James deals with this term in a short section in his chapter on Perception, and explains that he has not used it because of the very different meanings which have at various times attached to it.   It is a word with an eventful history, and played a great part in Kant's system.   We may perhaps say that what it meant for Kant was the modification produced in the matter of perception owing to the nature of the perceiving mind.   This is an attempt to do what has since been done more fully—to insist, that is, upon the activity of the mind

in perception, and to explain the nature of that activity. In this explanation the chief danger to be avoided is that of representing Apperception as some kind of innate faculty, in a sense approaching that of the old faculty-Psychology. For its modern or Herbartian meaning we may take Mr. Stout's definition of Apperception as " the process by which a mental system appropriates a new element, or otherwise receives a fresh determination." It is one case of blending, sometimes leading to the repro- duction of a former context ; but the term has special reference to the modifications which are produced in the new element by its incorporation with the old. In this respect it is not unlike Wundt's assimilation. It is important to remark that the old element itself may, or indeed *must*, be modified in the process. We cannot treat the old elements, the " apperceiving mass," as being entirely active, while the new element is entirely passive, and merely allows itself to be appropriated without exercising any influence on its appropriator. On this point James quotes from Steinthal as follows : " Although the *a priori* moment commonly shows itself to be the more powerful, Apperception-pro- cesses can perfectly well occur in which the new observation transforms or enriches the apperceiving groups of ideas. A child who hitherto has seen none but four-cornered tables apperceives a round one as a table, but by this the apperceiving mass ('table') is enriched. To his previous knowledge of tables comes this new feature, that they need not be four-cornered, but may be round." In this way the doctrine connects with that of Connotation and Denotation, illustrating the defectiveness of the view according to which they vary inversely ; by adding to the kinds of things *de*noted by a term, the child adds also to the qualities *con*noted by it.

This influence of the mind upon perception, which constitutes what is known as apperception, is capable of infinite illustration. The child who called a fern a "pot of green feathers" interpreted the novel object by an acquired disposition ; he saw what he had seen before, not what the country child would see. The different perceptions which different people will have of the same object can only be explained by the contents of their minds, which have interpreted the perception differently in each case. "On a particular occasion during the recent visit of the Empress of Germany to London it became the duty of the reporters of the public journals to describe Her Imperial Majesty's dress. *The Times* stated that the Empress was in 'gold brocade,' while according to the *Daily News* she wore a 'sumptuous white silk dress.' *The Standard*, however, took another view—'The Empress wore something which we trust it is not vulgar to call light mauve.' On the other hand, the *Daily Chronicle* was hardly in accord with any of the others—'To us it seemed almost a sea-green, and yet there was now a cream and now an ivory sheen to it.'" (Quoted from *Globe*, in Rooper on "Object-teaching.") It is the old truth, that "the eye can only see what it brings with it the power of seeing," expanded into a whole theory of mind. It may be illustrated in a wider way from the varying conceptions of history ; our "histories" are the offspring of our current interests.

The psychical elements which form the contents of the mind are so grouped and interconnected as to constitute what are technically known as Appercipient masses or systems. M. Paulhan (Stout's *Psychology*) compares this mental grouping to the organisation within a commonwealth. Some of the systems may be very simple, while others are very complex ; the simpler ones will be generally subordinate to the complex ones, and throughout there will be more or less interaction. Systems may compete with each other, they may also co-operate. They will compete when, and in so far as, they tend to exclude each other from contact with a given presentation ; difficulties in classifying any new object or " specimen " will be due to this rivalry between appercipient systems, or indecision as to which of two interests we will sacrifice. On the other hand they will co-operate in so far as they excite each other by some coherence between them. A system is strengthened in competition by the number of co-operating systems which are excited, so to say, *on its side*. By their adherence it gains in weight and interest, and gradually drives its rival from the field. Appercipient masses are the ideas which are more or less dominant *pro tem.*, and they will vary in prominence according to the interest before the mind, whether this interest be internally or externally originated. They " rise to the occasion."

Generic ideas are in this sense appercipient masses. By blending they reinforce that element of the presentation which has a common content with them, and the other elements which they do not share are thrust out of sight, unless some other appercipient mass is awakened to receive them.

As an instance of the way in which the dominant mass determines *what* content shall hold the field, we may note the effect of *context* in determining the interpretation we put upon words. The word "secular" has two meanings; and if it stands in isolation, there is no way of deciding what meaning is to be attached to it; probably the most common one will be suggested. But in reading the line "Through all the secular to be," the force of the context is so strong as not only to determine the meaning, but in some cases as to exclude even the suggestion of the alternative. The same is true of all words in so far as they are found in a living context, and not in the isolation of the spelling-book.

Not only may the systems of appercipient masses be *compared* to organisations of persons; they actually constitute their common mind and will. To say that certain persons have common interests means that in this or that respect their minds are similarly or correlatively organised, that they will react in the same or correlative ways upon given presentations. It is this identity of mental organisation which is the psychological justification for the doctrine of the General Will.

Passing from Apperception we come to Association. In philosophical interest it is subordinate to apperception, which is almost equivalent to the organised working of the mind, and this carries us to the higher stages of conscious life; but as the *machinery* of the mind Association is fundamental. The doctrine really dates from Plato (*Phaedo*, 73 *sq.*). His point is to bring the whole process of knowledge under the law of reproduction, in order to establish his ἀνάμνησις; it is the recovery by Association of mental possessions which we have lost. For him the process of reproduction is the same as that of knowledge. All given presentations act by suggestion, and therefore come under the general head of reproduction. In *Phaedo*, 76, he clearly indicates cases of association by contiguity and resemblance. " For we saw that this was possible : that when perceiving something, whether by sight or hearing or any other kind of sense, one may, from this perception, get a suggestion of something else which one had forgotten, to which the first mentioned was contiguous, though unlike, or to which it was like."

Aristotle, again, suggests as the laws of Association — Resemblance, Contrast, Co-existence, and Succession, or, combining the last two, Contiguity.

Contrast is now admitted to be a case of contiguity, and similarity remains as the great recent crux (see Bradley, *Logic*, and Ward, *l.c.*). It is a difficulty of principle. Similarity only exists when two ideas are before the mind, and therefore it cannot be used to reproduce one of those two. Moreover, it is only needed as an explanation if we regard images as simple ; if we admit that they are all complex, it can be reduced to contiguity (see Lecture II.). The given elements *abc* reproduce their former context by contiguity, and that former context persists and is compared with the given object. Take the case of the portrait, which Plato uses ; the portrait consists of elements *abcde*, the idea of the actual person consists of elements *abcfg*. The identical *abc* suggests *fg*, with which it is contiguous in the other context, and then the portrait is compared with the idea of the actual person.

James points out (*Text-Book*, p. 270) that there is no tendency to this recall by similarity amongst *simple* ideas ; it is only where complex ideas have an identical element that we find it. In what he calls "focalised recall," the active element, after awakening its new set of associates, *continues persistently active* along with them ; that is, it is an element identical in the two ideas.

Contiguity.—It is no doubt an improvement to reduce association to contiguity, as Ward and James have done ; but the question of the elements *between which* the contiguity or connection operates still remains. The principle that Association marries only universals has been discussed in dealing with Psychological Atomism. When the identical element in operation has a number of associates, what determines which will be recalled ? (See James, p. 264 ; Bradley, *Logic.*) It resolves itself into a question of apperception ; those associates which are in connection with the dominant appercipient system will be introduced, while others will be neglected.

The nature of identity is at the root of the question. We might represent it by a forked line Y; two lines having an identical part. Certainly it is not singularity (see Ward, *l.c.,* p. 81), for this excludes difference. The way in which the whole question of Atomism is here involved may be brought out by asking ourselves in what our ideal of knowledge consists. Is it "A is A," the mere repetition of the same concept ? or is it "man is animal," the connection of two concepts by an element common to both ?

The distinction has been drawn between material and individual identity, but perhaps it is not an ultimate one. Individual identity is one of content, in which we may treat a new beginning as constituting an essential difference or not, according to its laws of change.   If interruption in time is to be regarded as fatal to individual identity, what becomes of the identity of my mind, with its periodical lapses? or, again, of the House of Commons as an element in the British Constitution?

To sum up: All cognition is Identity asserting itself.

LECTURE V

SELF-CONSCIOUSNESS

1. *Its Relation to Consciousness.* — Regarded as phases in the development of mind, consciousness and self-consciousness are not strictly successive, although of course the higher tends to become predominant in the later stages of development. According to our view of self-consciousness, a savage must have his form of it (perhaps even the higher animals have something corresponding to it) in his feelings of success or of being equal to what has to be done. In quite an elementary stage of development we have the feeling of what is expected of us, or necessary, in order that the world may recognise us ; the feeling that finds expression, *e.g.*, in saying " Ça me connait " instead of " I know it."

2. *Its Relation to Cognition.*—Consciousness, on the whole, we have classed mainly under cognition ; it is necessarily a more one-sided state of mind than self-consciousness. As its type we took the Judgment of Perception ; or, on a large scale, Natural Science. The attitude of consciousness is : I *know* this object, which is *given*, which is simply contrasted with *me*. The subject in this state of mind

is very abstract, or indeed practically disappears; the *self* is felt rather than reflected on.

Self-consciousness has, of course, its cognitive side, but it can hardly be included under cognition. In explaining the origin even of consciousness, we had to take *action* into account, and this is still more the case with self-consciousness. When reflection is attracted to the self, which is more or less of a unity, the will cannot be disregarded, though in cognition we may perhaps abstract from it. As Science corresponds to Consciousness, so Philosophy corresponds to Self-consciousness; as compared with the abstract sciences it is a return to the concrete, and in it again we come nearer to the element of Will. It expresses the attitude of the self to experience, and in this sense experimental science has some affinity to it.

3. *The Element of Will.*—The general nature of self-consciousness is that it recognises itself as an object, which passes into recognising the object as itself. Consciousness keeps the two, the self and the object, distinct and apart (see James's *Analysis of the Self*). In producing this recognition the element of self-assertion is plainly operative. We may recall the effect ascribed to *disappointment* in generating consciousness; *successful* self-assertion against the object tends to produce the feeling that its independence or resistance is a sham, that it is not really alien. Indeed, as Hegel points out, we do not really believe that the objects of the external world exist in their own right, since we go so far as to eat and drink them. We have a parallel to this in Cognition when we discover that science,

"the reality of things," is, in fact, a system of thoughts. Then "otherness" takes a last refuge in the "Thing in itself," which is a mere thought; "we lift the curtain which hides the last recess, and find that there is nothing to be seen, unless, indeed, we go behind the curtain ourselves, both for the purpose of seeing and in order that there may be something to see" (Hegel, *Phenom.* p. 126). Then at last we recognise that all along this process has in some sense or another been within the self; that the object is not alien, but is always passing over into the self.

4. *The Recognition of Persons.*—Hegel illustrates the transition from Consciousness to Self-consciousness by a social evolution—that from slavery to civilised equality in a commonwealth. The important element to him is the element of recognition of another's personality, or of our own personality by another; and this in its lowest form exists as the result of a struggle, such as the struggle between slave and master. (Compare also the struggle between Beatrice and Benedick.) The slave, though in one sense a mere thing, is capable of recognition, and has accepted the position of subservience in such a way that he reflects his master's will or self-assertion, and thereby makes it aware of itself. Then by a long process of evolution this inequality is stripped off, until in a civilised commonwealth we have the reciprocal recognition of free individuals, in whom the same self-consciousness responds to itself, and constitutes a system of rights and duties and aims which is the positive substance of self-consciousness. If we compare self-consciousness in

E

the bad sense, we find that the term is used when the self is indeed aware of itself but cannot count upon a positive place, upon that definite recognition which constitutes its reality.   It is the *form* of self-consciousness without an adequate content. Speaking generally, it is only in the medium of recognition that a realised self-consciousness can exist; outside of this medium we get either the hero or the lunatic.   This is important for the theory of rights.

In recent Psychology this view is represented by the account of the self as a person (Ward, *l.c.*, p. 84), or of the social self (James).   It may be questioned how far the conflict with other selves, and recognition by them, are necessary to the psychological development of self-consciousness.   All that seems necessary in theory is collision against our object, with enough impression on it to mark it as "mine."   Is the *body*, as the source of pleasure and pain, sufficient for the purpose?   It is extraordinary how much it takes to start self-consciousness, especially in the absence of looking-glasses;[1] in the early part of a healthy life it hardly occurs to us that we have an appearance at all; and we shall find that it is usually the estimate of others, or our estimate of them, that suggests it.   A tiger, or even a savage, can only feel the effect of its own appearance from seeing its fellows.   Language, self-decoration, sexual selection, the family, everything which helps to fix the attention on those persistent presentation groups which are in definite relation with the self, must help.   To

---

[1] Cf. "*Cas.* Tell me, good Brutus, can you see your face?
Brut. No, Cassius; for the eye sees not itself,
But by reflection, by some other things."

sum up : Self-consciousness, *as we experience it*, is for the most part social.

5. *The Meanings of Self.*—James makes a useful distinction between " I " and " me " ; the self as knower and the self as known. The known self or me he distinguishes again into the *material me, the social me,* and *the spiritual me.* These are not so much phases as different aspects of the developed self, an analysis of what can be called " mine " into divisions which correspond roughly to (i.) property or products, (ii.) reputation, (iii.) mind. All that is in any sense mine goes to make up the me, and from the first more is mine than my own body. Perhaps also less. According to James our social selves are other people's ideas of us ; but to this we should add that they are other people's ideas of us *as reflected into our own ideas.* These analyses are very important for questions of altruism and egoism, and we shall have more to say of them. But if we compare pp. 184, 194, 195, we shall find that James does not make full use of his analyses. He comes to use the expressions " bodily self-seeking " and " egoism " quite uncritically, in the vulgar sense ; forgetting, *e.g.*, that the material or bodily me, as he has described it, would include quite impersonal results, such as an artist's pictures.

Ward's analysis is perhaps more difficult. He distinguishes *the Bodily Self, the Inner Self,* and *the Self as Person.* These are more like phases than elements, and we may note that he uses the expression " first of all " in speaking of the *Bodily Self.* But from the first the core of experiences identified with feeling probably includes more than the body group; it includes whatever has not been separated by special division, such as experiences of the home and family, and there seems no reason to think that these would be sifted out as we go back to more primitive stages where discrimination is less. Of course we must not think of an accurate perception of our bodies at an early stage: that develops with the spatial discrimination of objects in general.

The *Inner Self* (see also Sully)[1] seems to be the mind considered as a thing inside the body, like the ghost or soul which the savage believes in, and located perhaps in the breast, where emotion seems to be felt. There is a difficulty in distinguishing between content and locality. The Homeric Greek says, " I too have a mind fashioned in my breast, in no way defective." He identifies the *seat* of mind with that of emotional disturbance, but the content of his self—his body and arms and ancestry and actions—is not confined to this mind-thing. Here we have the germ of the distinction between the Psychological and Logical point of view. The savage *has* his mind; it is not his whole world, but a thing, a *part* of himself, just as he has eyes and ears and feet, and a certain character or fame.

True Self-consciousness begins with the *Self as a Person*, as we have explained it above. It is characterised, as Ward says, by the not-self reacting upon the self; *i.e.* by reciprocal recognition in which the not-self becomes a second self with a corresponding appercipient group. A person is a subject of rights and duties, and is aware of his own qualities as conditioning his own rights and duties: " I *am* a workman or teacher," etc.

[1] *Human Mind*, i. 477.

Altruism and the Self.—If we look at what Sully says of the reflected self in children we find that, as also in James, the contrast of extra-regarding impulses and self-love seems inconsistent with our conception of the self, and very confusing. The writers seem to oscillate between the " mind-thing " inside the body and the content of the mind, which includes, *e.g.*, our family. We must ask to *what* self are the extra-regarding impulses external? According to our answer to this we get exactly opposite views of their nature.

The general form of Self-consciousness is Reflection or " Internal Perception," and this corresponds to James's Spiritual Self. It is expressed as " This is my thought, or will, or feeling," of which the central core is " This is my idea of myself," and " I am I " ; thus it is always empirical.

This implies the distinction between the self which knows and the self which is known ; James's distinction between " I " and " me." There are three matters in which his account—which is very good— needs emphasising.

(i.) The Self as Me (= all that is mine) includes the object and relative not-me as well as the subject. It is the whole of my mental contents ; for of course the matters about which I habitually think modify my individuality and fall within my mind. It is important to distinguish my self as = " mine," including my past self and the self which I repudiate, from self as the momentary subject in knowledge or action. There seems to be a tendency in Ward to cut down the self towards the subject; and James's classification is not quite distinct, *e.g.*, as to the line between the material self and the social self. My family is in the former, and I as reflected in the minds of my family am in the latter. But what he aims at is including in the self all that in any way belongs to me, is " mine."

(ii.) Within the me or mine, the relative " not-me " and the " I " have to a great extent interchangeable contents. What is mine is a fluctuating material (James). Our current course of ideas, *e.g.*, may jar with some distinct line of thought which we wish to pursue ; then we fight against it, and it thereby becomes a relative " not-me " within the " mine," just as much as the noise of a barrel-organ. Again, we may stand aside from our past self, and pass judgment upon it (Ward) : " I was not my self when I did that." Even the elements in our present emotional state we may set over against us as objects, and say they are wrong, they ought to be otherwise ; that is, there is some group of contents, some feeling and idea, which becomes one with our innermost core, and reacts against the elements of our present emotional state. Then this group of contents is the " I," and the present emotional state, though within the " me," is relatively to it the " not-me."

This is not so hard as it seems ; it is simply the way in which we handle our experience. There is no doubt that within our whole mental content there is a continual fluctuation between the "I" and "me" and " not-me." We really can take the self to be almost anything in our experience, and in the same way we can regard anything in our experience as our not-self ; we are somewhat differently identified with every change of attention. For instance, I may feel myself an extension lecturer, and as such criticise the regular University teachers, or *vice versa*. Or again, I may contrast my holiday life and town life ; when I am in the one, I criticise the other ; or to take an example of the same thing within a smaller circuit, I may criticise *my self as I think I am at the moment*, *e.g.* as I am in my holiday life. By analysing what I feel my self to be, I drag it out to be looked at, and in so doing pass over as much of the self as I can, from the subject into the object ; the " I " passes into the " me " and the "not-me."

(iii.) In Psyschology, then, the " I " is not the pure or abstract ego ; that is a mere abstraction of the attribute of knowing. The "I" in Psychology is always accompanied by content, and this content is not permanent or unchangeable, or essentially attached to the self.

6. This brings us to the question of Personal Identity (see James, pp. 201 *sq.*). In discussing it the principle to follow is, that it is of the same nature as the identity of any other thing ; *i.e.* that it does not exclude change, and can only be stated relatively to some purpose.

For practical purposes, *e.g.* in law, we go in the main by bodily identity ; but this is at once sub-jected to reservations, and bodily identity is only regarded as a *sign* of personal identity, not as con-stituting it. There is a difficulty in speaking of the " same mind," since the mind does not *seem* to have continuous existence. Great psychological interest attaches to those qualities which bind experiences together into a single experience, in spite of changes and interruptions ; the basis consists of bodily feeling, and—as James points out—a mass of identical elements which, though they alter, do not as a rule all alter at once. But identity does not depend upon the individual's *sense* of *unity* in his experience or memory, for this may be false ; it is not memory, but only the facts as truly remembered that seem to make actual identity. The abstract " I " or supposed pure ego will not help us, for identity must be a content, something that we take to be essential ; a pure form can have neither identity nor change. James deals with limiting cases in his account of morbid egos. The basis of self-feeling (bodily sensations, etc.) being cut in two, reproduction cannot produce it as a single experience ; *a* brings up *bcd*, and *β* brings up *efg*, but *a* and *β* with their respective associations exclude each other.

Practically, our result is that the question cannot be answered *in general ;* there is no essential in-dividual, and no essence apart from a teleological point of view. We must define our question by a statement of purpose : Is this man still the same in *intellect*, in *character*, in his *legal obligations*, or in *nationality ?*—then we can find a definite answer. The practical fact that removes any grave difficulty is, that though we may say that a man ceases to be himself, we have as a rule no reason to raise the question as to whether he can become some one else who already exists. Our system of responsibility would be seriously shaken if bodily identity were no longer a sufficient guide ; if, that is, I could enter your body to do something wrong, and then return, as has been suggested in cases of hypnotism.

7. *Feeling in Self.*—All the elements of the " I," the " me," and the relative " not-me," are always held together by *feeling*, of which the nucleus is probably

the somatic consciousness with its pleasure and pain. This feeling is qualified by everything which falls into the background of consciousness. Our clothing, the habitual surroundings of our room, warmth and cold, habits and recollections,—myriads of things like these keep up a habitual feeling of one's particular life. This is always present more or less in all that we do or think, and it is what, empirically speaking, maintains our sense of continuity. We all know how in some mode of life which we take up intermittently a special continuity forms itself: we fall into the ways of the place or people, and feel as if we had never been away. This comes from the innumerable details which modify the background of feeling, and so reinstate the particular self that belongs to the life there. How far we might be broken up by an absolute change and clean cut from the past is not often tried, but we get an approach to it in some cases of so-called "double personality," or even of "conversion."

Analogous to this, but more reflective, is self-feeling in the sense of a special emotion such as pride or vanity. This supervenes upon the whole structure of personality, instead of forming the base of it, but there is no doubt that it acts to some extent in the same way as bodily and general feeling in strengthening the feeling of continuous personality.

LECTURE VI

FEELING has many kindred terms in our vocabulary, such as passion, affection, emotion, and sensation. Sensation, however, has now acquired a somewhat different meaning, in which it is generally used ; and all originally indicated more of passivity or receptiveness. We may see what a curious change has taken place in the usage of the terms by comparing *passionate* or *affectionate* with *passive* or *affected* in the sense of being easily affected by pity or the weather or the like. " Passionate " or " in a passion ' we should now consider to be a very active state. " Feeling," though originally about equivalent to " passion," has retained its passive sense ; πάθος is Greek for " passion or feeling " ; πάσχειν or *pati* means to suffer, to have something happen to you. Emotion, again, seems to indicate a condition of activity as the result of being acted upon, *i.e.* of passivity (cf. French *s'émouvoir*).

Sensation seems to be meant for an active form, although it is not a true derivative from any verb. It *has* even been used popularly of states that belong to feeling in the narrowest sense, *i.e.* of pleasure and pain ; and it still has a peculiar use for a shocking or striking emotion, as when we speak of a sensation novel or a sensation in court. But on the whole it is now used, especially in Psychology, to indicate something belonging to cognition ; a mental element referred to one or other of the definite five senses (probably from analogy with the word *sense*). Then, again, feeling is used for one special kind of sensation, *touch*, and sometimes also for other sensations which are not easily classified, *e.g.* for warmth and cold, for the sensation experienced during the motions of the limbs, and for the organic sensations. This is perhaps due to a tendency to regard the less definite contents as "feeling," this being the more general term.

It will help us to understand the use of these terms if we say a few words as to their history. The connection of *Feeling*, in the sense of *emotion*, with passiveness probably came from the idea of Reason as being the essential activity of mind, for this led to the emotional states being regarded as forced upon the mind from without and, as it were, upsetting it ; they were always looked upon as *given*, not inferred or made.

It was this comparison and contrast between "feelings" and intelligence which struck Descartes and his school, by whom they were treated as "confused modes of thought." One characteristic of the so-called feelings is certainly brought out by this way of describing them, *i.e.* that they are distinguishable amongst each other by reason of a content or object. If, for instance, we consider the difference between Anger and Fear, we find it to consist in our relation towards a certain evil. Perhaps, also, it is true that *during* an emotion the content is not usually clear ; a man could not or would not analyse his emotion while undergoing it ; and then in a sense it is obscure. But there is always something more than the content and its obscurity to be taken account of ; the theory failed to explain the *peculiar* nature of feeling, its aspect as to pleasure and pain.

In modern times Kant was the first to definitely place this "feeling of pleasure and pain" on an independent basis as a third capacity of the soul, neither cognitive nor appetitive (*Kritik der r. Verumft*, p. 16). This is the current view of to-day, and we shall return to it directly ; the difficulty of the transition to it is that our "feelings" are not exactly modification or species of "feeling" itself in the strict sense.

Just at Kant's time there was an outburst of a view contrary to his, which was partly owing to his "agnostic" tendency. Jacobi, for instance, following Rousseau, was impressed by the apparent reality and depth of Feeling (as when we speak of religious or poetic feeling), and regarded it as an organ of spiritual truth ; thus placing it *above* reflective know-ledge, and not *below*, as Descartes had done. This is an important contribution to the conception of Feeling ; it lays stress on its directness or immediate-ness, through which it seems to give us a contact with reality that nothing else does, and at the same time it agrees with the older view in insisting on *content*, *i.e.* that *something positive* (I do not say *definite*) seems to be brought home to us in Feeling. It is, indeed, somewhat of a paradox ; you have a grasp of something, but cannot say of what. Some-times Jacobi called this faculty Reason, but for him

it was always direct and unreflective, and superior
to reflection. It is important to note that great
attention was being paid to æsthetic philosophy at
this time.

Now of course the great idealists could not let
Feeling stand above Reason—no systematic philosopher could ; nevertheless this view, vehemently as it
was attacked by Hegel, did affect his own theory.
He insists, that is, on the directness and reality of
Feeling ; all content has to pass through the form
of Feeling, and in that sense it might be said that
Feeling is the one revelation of reality. But then
it is only the *beginning* or germ, it is *what you are*
psychically, not *what you know;* its contents are
dragged out one by one and made objective and
systematic, and without this process of interpretation
it gives no definite results. Hence in using it as
evidence of anything we are interpreting it, putting
a meaning into it. It is, of course, a form of
experience which must not be neglected ; but
whether we give it the name of Feeling or not, is
a merely verbal matter. Whatever we may call
it, this " immediate " phase of mind is the germ both
of intellect and of will.

The modern view (say that of Ward) on the
whole goes back to that of Kant. Feeling, according
to this view, is the pure feeling of pleasure or pain ;
it cannot be identified with either cognition or
volition, and does not, as such, include any " matter "
or " content." Upon the relation of these aspects
to the whole psychosis or mental state, the student
should read Ward's article carefully (*l.c.*, p. 44) ; we
have not three kinds of state, but three characters
or features, in the whole mental state at any moment.

It follows from this that what we popularly call a *feeling* or *emotion*—such as hope, anger, etc.—is really made up of (i.) pure Feeling, *i.e.* a degree of pleasure or pain, and (ii.) elements of presentation, of sensation or cognition, which are accompanied by this pure Feeling.

Pure Feeling, then, in this limited sense has no quality. The quality or character of what is generally called a feeling or emotion comes from the sensations or cognitions that go with it. For instance, in a burning pain or a gnawing pain, the qualities of burning or gnawing are *sensations ;* the pain is distinct from them, and is said to be separable and slower in arising. The only characteristics belonging to pain and pleasure as such are intensity and rhythm ; so that a throbbing pain may perhaps take the quality of throbbing from the rhythm of the pain itself. This agreeable or disagreeable accompaniment of a sensation is called its "tone," and it seems probable that all sensations have in some degree this tone, although it is often hardly perceptible.

This account, taken in connection with the fact that there is no sign of a separate set of nerve-centres for the emotions or for pleasure and pain, seems to go a long way towards settling the question whether pure Feeling is an object of cognition, *i.e.* whether it is a presentation.

If the question were : " Are warmth and cold, or sweetness and bitterness, or joy and fear presentations ? " the answer must be yes ; and it is difficult to see how we can exclude from the answer their respective accompaniments of pleasure and pain, for these certainly do make a difference to them. But if we ask: "Is the pleasure in sweetness or joy a separable element, like taste or form or colour, so that it can be perceived by itself as a positive object?" the answer must probably be no. At any rate it is clear what is meant; if I say "it is hot," or "it is red," I convey a perception to the hearer; but if I say "it is pleasant," I convey no perception of a special content. Perhaps the same may be said of such qualities as beautiful or ugly, cheerful or sombre; at any rate the abstraction seems to give rise to a difficulty in such cases. The prevalent opinion seems to be that the positive characters are perceived and not the feeling, but that the two are confused. It will be enough here just to state the counter question as to whether this is a fair account of all the predicates which imply agreeable and disagreeable feelings, whether they do not really objectify pleasure and pain *in their connection with presentative elements*. We certainly cannot have a pure Feeling, *i.e.* pleasure or pain, without qualities—so much seems clear. Feeling *in this sense* is nothing which constitutes a separate object by itself.

The next question which arises is that of the *conditions* of pleasure and pain.

It is natural for the theory of Evolution to take the view that pleasure goes with benefit to the organism, and pain with injury, for otherwise how could creatures have lived? The difficulty arises when we consider the obvious exceptions to this rule; Lotze, for instance, takes the case of a sweet poison, and points out that *feeling* only reports the immediate and local effect, and neglects consequences.

We need, then, to ask in what form benefit accompanies pleasure. Ward distinguishes between (i.) the Intensity and (ii.) the Quality of sensations ; and holds the view that (i.) Sensation as such is pleasant, while its *intensity* can be adequately met by attention, (ii.) that pleasant *quality* accompanies an expanding field of consciousness, and painful quality its contraction.

With regard to (ii.) we may raise the question of the relativity of pain and pleasure. Does pleasure essentially require the sense of conquering something that opposes it, so that it consists in the sense of victory ? If so, then contraction should certainly be painful, but it is not clear that it always is so, as, for instance, in going to sleep. Bradley suggests that it is not contraction as such, but discord, which is painful ; we do not feel that we lose unless there are some elements left to remind us of what we lose.

We may perhaps reduce the whole account to (i.), and say that Presentation is in itself pleasant when there is no discord. Then we shall regard pleasure as not *essentially* relative, *i.e.* as not essentially consisting in the removal of pain. Plato seems to have been right in admitting that there *are* relative pleasures, while asserting that there are also pure pleasures (such as the pleasures of smell, or æsthetic and intellectual pleasures). The question may also take a form in which it is the root of modern pessimism : Is pain the positive feeling, and pleasure only negative, *i.e.* a release from pain ? Schopenhauer took the view that this was so. The theory finds support in certain examples in which the same actual states —say of an illness—may be painful at one time and pleasant at another—painful after health, pleasant after worse illness ; but these cases may be quite well explained without making all pleasure purely

relative.   Plato's instances mentioned above retain
their weight ; there are pleasures which have no
pain preceding them.

We may say, then, that Pleasure seems to accompany all presentation which is not discordant, while
pain accompanies discord.   This really covers what
the old view meant by connecting pleasure with *activity*
(*i.e.* not motion but simply mental being), but differs
seriously from the view that pain checks activity.
We might rather say that pleasure is a stable condition, a condition of equilibrium, while pain is an
unstable condition seeking to regain equilibrium.[1]

We have said that most sensations, if not all, have
their *tone*, *i.e.* their pleasurable or painful accompaniment.   The same is true of probably every idea,
or interpretation of direct presentation; and the most
marked type of these ideas with their pleasurable or
painful accompaniments we call emotions.   James
describes these in his text-book, but they are really
individual in their nature, and a mere description is
not of much value.   Their distinctive quality, that by
which they differ, is all presentative ; the pure feeling,
or pleasure and pain, by which they are accompanied, is not to be got at by analysis, and must
be taken as being one throughout all of them.

The presentative elements in emotion may be
said on the whole to be of two kinds, ideal content
and bodily sensation (or bodily resonance).   James's
view is that there is, indeed, nothing else in the
emotion ; and there is, as we have said, no sign of a
separate emotional centre.   In fear, *e.g.*, the ideal
content is an evil menacing the self (in one sense

---

[1] Cf. Bradley in *Mind*, Jan. 1888, pp. 1-36, and Leslie Stephen,
Science of Ethics, p. 51.

or another of the self) ; the bodily resonance comes from a number of typical movements which have their own appropriate sensations, and which all combine in qualifying the painful feeling and together make up the peculiar recognisable psychosis, or state of mind, which we call fear. (The origin of these movements is historically interesting, but not of much philosophical value.) This view leads to three results about ideal feelings or emotions.

(i.) *In general* they can be analysed only in respect of their presentative elements (this recalls the point of view from which they are regarded as " confused ideas ").

(ii.) It has a particular bearing upon *Æsthetic Emotions.* What we call the expression of an emotion is really a modification of it, because it changes the external presentative elements contained in it. This modification may change the emotion in very important ways, and may even affect the ideal content itself. For the æsthetic emotions especially this view is fundamental ; for we may fairly say of them that they have to become such as can be embodied in an individual object, and this can only be by undergoing modification in their expression.

(iii.) *The Moral Emotions.*—In the ideal presentative element of an emotion—what we call its occasion or content—the central point is its relation to the self, and if we start from psychical individualism we tend to confuse emotions which are really quite opposite. We may illustrate this by the moral emotion of sympathy, for which the view is very important.

(*a*) Sympathy may be an emotion arising from the

contagion of feeling. I see you suffering pain, and I both feel a sympathetic pain and more or less reflect upon what such a pain would be to me, to my sensitive self. The content of the emotion is then my sensitive self related to a pain like yours, and this pain is the object of the emotion just as the threatened evil is the object of fear. This is the elementary form of sympathy; it is to feel with another in the sense of feeling the same as he feels, *i.e.* if he is pained I am pained, but not necessarily because he is anything to me. It is "with him," but not "for him." No doubt this form of the emotion rests upon the fact of a common nature, but it does not involve the recognition of it, and for Ethics this is all-important.

(β) Sympathy, on the other hand, may be the direct consequence of a wide self, of a recognition of unity between ourselves and others, or even between ourselves and nature. More truly we should say it is due to the absence of a discrimination between us and others, for we must here deny the starting-point of individualism entirely. Our connection with others is, so to speak, in the Self, and not in the Not-self; and from this point of view the whole content of the feeling of sympathy is quite different. It does not come round through the sensitive self at all. To a parent the care of the child's body is as direct an object as the care of his own. It is not that he is uneasy because he feels the same pain that the child feels, but that the idea of the child's pain is at once the idea of an evil attacking himself.

To take a purely imaginary instance, let us suppose that there is a newspaper attack on our

particular University Extension centre.   Putting
aside the direct personal irritation caused in each
of us separately by the attack, how should we feel
it sympathetically ?

(i.) We should feel it in the first place by mere
contagion ; that is, we should, as sensitive individuals,
tend to feel the same that the other members of the
centre are feeling.[1]   The external signs of their
vexation would make us realise more vividly the
idea of the attack, and would suggest vexation to
ourselves.   This feeling in each of us would be *with*
the others, but not necessarily *for* them; it would be
a repetition of their feeling in us, and not a new
feeling in which they were regarded as persons to be
considered.   This form of "sympathy" is purely
selfish, and is not the most original or natural form.

(ii.) We *ought* also to feel what is quite different,
that the attack was an injury to an embodied purpose which is an element of our own ideal selves,
and in respect of which we are all so far one.   Then
the regret or resentment of each one of us would be
direct, and would be directly *for* all, because of the
evil threatening the ideal self, which includes the
other persons in so far as they are concerned in the
organisation.   There *need* not be any sympathy in
the sense of intensifying one's own personal vexation
by attending to the personal vexation of the others ;
the pain would accompany a discord, not in the
private sensitive self, but in the larger ideal self.

When we come to speak of Altruism and Egoism
these distinctions are important.   Take as another
instance the sympathy between members of a family.
If any one injures or insults your wife or child, the

[1] Cf. Ward, *l.c.*, on Egoistic and Social feelings.

content of your emotion is not the idea of a painful state in your private self *like* that which has been caused in your wife or child, but the idea of an evil directly attacking one element of your ideal and wider self, with its consequent pain and resentment. There is no going round through your own private pain except in so far as it is necessary in order to understand what has happened; but that is only a question as to how you form the idea of the injury, not as to why you resent it. We find similar instances of sympathetic feeling in such organisations as the Church or Trade Unions, in so far as they form an element common to the selves of the individuals comprised in them.

LECTURE VII

1. *Ideomotor Action.*—There is one theory according to which all Volition is treated as a modification, or particular application, of what is known as " ideomotor action " (see James's chapter on Will). As it is useful to master a distinct view, even if it strikes us at first as paradoxical, we will discuss this first ; other views can then be presented by contrast with it or in modification of it.

Every one agrees that in Volition there is present an idea, which first goes beyond fact and is then followed by fact in conformity with it. We might almost say that the idea is at first " conflicting with fact," but that this would not include certain cases of continued action or position. For instance, in the volition of the soldier who stands still to be shot at, the idea (that of continuing to stand) goes beyond the present, but does not conflict with it.

In many forms of action there is nothing psychical involved but this idea, which goes beyond fact ; in hypnotic suggestion, *e.g.*, where the idea fills the mind to the exclusion of everything else ; or in action consequent upon " fixed ideas," or in any form of conscious associative suggestion, as when I go to a bookshelf for a book which I want, see another and am prompted by the idea of its contents to take it down and begin reading it, to the entire exclusion of the first. Carpenter in his *Mental Physiology*, chap. vi., even includes in such ideomotor action *unrecognised* cases of volition, such as take place in the use of the divining-rod ; but he describes them as " reflex actions of the cerebrum," and does not regard them as instances of Will at all. Imitative movements may also be regarded, at any rate in many cases, as instances of ideomotor action ; and these to a great extent fall into the category of actions which are ordinarily called voluntary.[1] In the lower ideomotor actions (such as hypnotic action) the subject is unaware that the action proceeds from the idea ; but at a rather higher level—that, *e.g.*, of fixed ideas—he is aware of it.

These are all more or less abnormal cases, but it is possible to take Ideomotor action as the typical case of Will, and to lay down the principle that every idea which can suggest action tends to pass into action ; *i.e.* that it passes into action if not checked by some counteracting idea or by pain. In Ideomotor action of this kind we are fully aware that the idea is fulfilling itself. Then, as James says, the Will consists only in attention to the idea ; it passes into action without further interference on our part. Indeed, the idea, according to this view, simply *is* the sign of a nascent action which may be checked or may proceed to completion. Or we may stop short of the principle that consciousness is in this way itself *motor*, and merely extend the principle of Association and say that it exists between ideas

[1] See Sully, *Human Mind*, vol. ii. pp. 214, 244, and Ward, *l.c.* p. 43.

and the physical states which accompany them; then it will be possible for an idea to call up an appropriate action as the means to realise itself, just as an idea may call up another idea.

As examples of how Volition is treated on this view, we may take :—

(i.) *Internal Volition.*—This is the simplest case, as it dispenses with the question of muscular contractions. Take as a special instance that of a lecturer haunted by the idea of treating the subject of Volition in a lecture—the abstract idea of preparing a certain subject for an occasion. All sorts of distractions tend to come up in his mind, business matters, amusements, etc. ; but the idea of a certain definite treatment of Volition persists and holds its own against distractions, and develops into subdivisions and reflections, until at last it has become a mental fact conforming to the abstract idea with which he started. In other words, the idea has produced a mental reality corresponding to its content : expressed formally, *a* has passed into A. Of course such a mental operation as this is much helped in practice by making notes, etc., and here we pass into muscular contraction, but this is not essential to the volition. Think for instance of what takes place when you do a bit of mental arithmetic. You start, say, with an abstract idea of the cost of building a house ; certain data are given to work from, these suggest their combinations in your mind, and at last the result, a definite figure, becomes a mental fact; you started from *a* and attain *A*. In short, the theory is summed up in the words: it is will when an idea produces facts conformable to it,[1]

[1] Bradley, *l.c.*

and in this way modern Psychology is taking us right back to Socrates.

(ii.) In *External Volition* the elements, for normal cases, are just the same. There is first the anticipation of a *movement* or *external effect*, or it may be of both—*e.g.* the thought of starting to come down to the lecture-hall (*a*); and secondly, the perception of the motion as actually taking place (A). The first element is simply a reproduced idea due to previous experience of the second, and there seems no reason to suppose that motor impulses, as such, are felt at all. What happens is that some stimulus or perception—*e.g.* of the time—suggests the idea of motion, and the idea of motion then passes into its reality.

The question naturally arises as to how on this view we are to distinguish Volition from Expectation. In Expectation we have the same two elements, the anticipation followed by the result, but they are not connected in the same way. That is to say, in Expectation there is some connection, other than the anticipatory idea, which we know to be the operative link bringing about the result. There is present to the mind *a* and *A*, but there is also the knowledge that if the cause of A is to be represented another element must be taken into account; the *process* is *b* and A. When we expect the clock to strike, the sound, as it occurs, is immediately referred to an external cause (*b*). But when we do think our idea is connected with the result, then Will is present, even though the connection may really be altogether different. Norna in Scott's *Pirate* wills that her song shall stop the storm, and the storm stops; just as the spiritualist wills the table to cross the room to him, and the table comes. If they had *only expected* the result, they would have attributed it to some external cause (*b*).

Is there something more than the persistent idea itself required to constitute volition? There is no doubt that we are accustomed to think of an act of will as involving something like a *fiat*, or *effort ;* but we can more easily consider the nature of this in connection with the idea of *activity*, and after dealing with *attention.*

The question has been raised as to the origin of Will—whether, *e.g.*, it has been developed from reflex action. It would perhaps be better to say that *all* action is a modified reflex, in the sense that it is sensation plus motion ; but it does not seem likely that fixed reflexes pass into volition, while instances are common of actions originally "voluntary" becoming through habit reflex, or " secondarily automatic." [1]

2. According to the view we have been considering Will depends upon Attention to an idea ; and that brings us to the question, what is *Attention ?* [2]

At first sight the matter seems so simple as to call for no explanation ; we all know what we mean by *attending* to anything. But the governing difficulty here, as in the question of Free-will and all kindred questions of activity, is to explain the *relevancy* of the attention. " *I* am actively attending," you say ; yes, but in attending you are selecting, and why, or how, do you select one thing rather than another to which to attend? To refer to activity, choice, or even muscular preparation, does not help

[1] Cf. Ward, p. 43, and Sully, *Human Mind*, vol. ii. pp. 191, 192.
[2] Cf. James, pp. 221, 222; Ward, *l.c.* p. 41, col. 2; Bradley, " Activity of Attention," *Mind*, 1886, p. 341.

us at this point; it is only giving another name to
the same fact. It is tension of the ear, you say,
which enables me to attend to, or hear, the note;
but tension to *which* note? Unless you can show
how and why one element in particular attracts or
fixes your will or attention at a particular moment,
it seems to become a matter of chance; and if chance,
there is no selection or volition. James introduces
the conception of Free-will to solve the difficulty
(p. 237). " No object can *catch* our attention " he
says, " except by the neural machinery. But the
amount of the attention which an object receives after
it has caught our mental eye is another question.
It often takes effort to keep the mind upon it. We
feel that we can make more or less of the effort as
we choose. If this feeling be not deceptive, if our
effort be a spiritual force, and an indeterminate one,
then, of course, it contributes co-equally with the
cerebral conditions to the result."

But to the psychologist this explanation is not
satisfactory (as indeed James seems to allow); it is
at best a mere miraculous loading of the scales, and
if so why should it not load them in the wrong
direction? It would be as if we cherished a capri-
cious demon somewhere in our nervous system, who
would now and again put his hand on the balance of
motives without any special relevance or reason. It
is this same want of relevance which was the radical
flaw in the Faculty doctrine. We can see this by
contrasting it with our idea of the self as constituted
by appercipient masses, which enables us to say
what gives its force to each element attended to,
while the idea of Faculties breaks up the mental
system into disconnected parts.

Attention, then, if it is to be relevant to the contents of consciousness, must be an effect of the Interest, or given Intensity, attaching to those contrasts. Of these two aspects we must note that as the appercipient masses develop, Interest tends to gain in effectiveness—*i.e.* to attract more attention—while Intensity tends to lose. We attend to sensations less because they are loud or vivid, and more because they are connected with many thoughts and experiences, so that the small and scarcely perceptible scratches of a familiar handwriting may for a time entirely exclude all the bustle of daily life around us. It is true that a loud report like that of firearms usually engages the attention, but that may be due as much to the idea of danger as to the intensity of the noise; moreover, as James points out, all voluntary attention is derivative, in the sense that in what we feel to be voluntary attention a perception is not forced upon us from without, but a dominant idea within forces upon us some perception connected with it. Much of our passive attention also has a *transferred* or *acquired* interest ; the postman's knock catches the ear quicker than another because of the letter he brings ; as in volition we are aware of the operative idea first going beyond the present and then realized, *a* and then A. Put into general terms, Attention = the working of Interest in selecting presentations, and Interest = the relation of presentations to the system of appercipient masses, with their concomitant feelings.

3. We may now return to the question of the so-called Fiat of Will, or the consciousness of activity in volition. The core of it would seem, at first sight,

to be the feeling of the motor impulse; but it is very doubtful whether this, as a special feeling, exists. That is to say, the difference in feeling of lifting a light weight and lifting a heavy weight seems upon analysis to be merely a difference in the sensations coming *in* from the muscles, and not to imply any feeling emanating from the centre. We feel ourselves active, as we explained above, when the idea *a* persists, and a change in the not-Self bringing with it A is referred to its persistence. Where this reference is not made, as in the use of the divining-rod, etc., we protest that we are *not* active. In cases of deliberative action at a high level of consciousness, the self or personality participates;[1] *i.e.* one of the ideas which are striving for predominance reinforces itself by the whole mass of our positive personality— purposes, associations, and feelings. As a rule the idea thus reinforced wins, and the self prevails against that which *ipso facto* becomes the not-self. This is really the answer to Sully's objection that " Ideomotor action—that is, the tendency to carry out an action merely because this is vividly suggested —is obviously not only useless but likely to be positively injurious."[2] Of course, if the action is vividly suggested only because all other considerations, *e.g.* of consequences, are excluded, the tendency is likely to be injurious; but if the " me " is taken into account—if, that is, the suggestion is vivid because reinforced by the whole moral self—that is the best security we can have of its sanity.

This is, in its general outlines, the theory of Volition as explained by analogy to Ideomotor

[1] Cf. Münsterberg, *Die Willenshandlung*, pp. 147, 148.
[2] Sully, *Human Mind*, vol. ii. p. 244.

action such as we have in Fixed Ideas, Hypnotic Suggestion, or Imitation. It is a theory which is easily understood, and has much experience in its favour; and it is completely opposed to the theory which represents the will as the last appetite before action. On the other hand we must note that some psychologists prefer to draw a sharp distinction between ideomotor action and volition, on the ground that the former does not necessarily involve a choice between conflicting alternatives.[1]

4. The further question which arises is twofold: Is Desire necessary to Will? and Does Pleasure really constitute the object of Desire?

(i.) *Is Desire necessary to Will?*—Desire seems upon analysis to involve three elements. If we delay the satisfaction of a normal appetite, say of hunger, then we get a fair instance of desire. Pure appetite *may* have no distinct object before it, in which case it is hardly desire; instinct goes straight to the movement without the intervention of ideas. But where there is delay to satisfy hunger we get the *idea of eating*, which is *felt* as pleasant, over against a *real absence of food*, which is painful, the whole complex state being pleasant or painful according to circumstances. The prospect of further delay may cause the pain to predominate, while the announcement of dinner may change the whole state to one of pleasure.

Thus there is no desire without the element of "uneasiness," due to the absence of the thing desired. Is this element discoverable in all cases of Will? The chief use of such questions is to make us realise

[1] Cf. Stout, *Psychology*, vol. i. p. 131.

their meaning ; the answer depends very much upon
what we include in the term Will. There are certain
kinds of Ideomotor action in which we believe we
are not active; *i.e.* hypnotic suggestions and imitative
movements and fixed ideas must in some cases be
excluded from Will. Fixed ideas, for instance, even
if conscious, may lead to actions which our self
would repudiate if fully aware of them ; our personality seems not fully awake, and we do not have a
fair chance of controlling them. Many, again, would
say that they cannot understand Voluntary action
apart from the effect of Pleasure at least, if not of
Pleasure and Pain. It is clear, then, that the answer
to the question whether Will involves Desire must
depend upon what kinds of action we regard as
voluntary. But before going on to consider the
object of Desire we may point out that in some
cases where volition is *most* deliberate, the element
of desire seems most conspicuously absent. When,
for instance, we approach a very important decision,
such as changing our residence or profession, or
taking a particular line in any kind of policy, for
which we have weeks or months in which to prepare,
in such cases as these we can hardly be said to
verify Desire. Our decision is more like a necessity
gradually revealing itself. Even if we have intervals
of pain or uneasiness with reference to the prospect,
it is very doubtful whether they determine the
decision ; it is more like a process by which a
certain prospective course exhibits itself as the only
solution of a certain problem, and so becomes more
and more dominant in the mind. Everything brings
us back to that particular course, or, as we say,
everything points that way. The fact is that

volition of this type tends to approximate to the mere choice of means, and this, it may be said, is not volition at all.   But when the so-called means actually qualify the end (*e.g.* the end of organising your life in accordance with certain standards), then it really is volition.   Suppose that you have to decide between going into Parliament and going into the Church ; both may be pleasant to you, and both afford opportunities of usefulness, and you will probably decide according to which seems most likely to be useful, taking into consideration your own particular powers.   The actual feeling accompanying the decision, or act of will, *might* be more like that of being absorbed in an idea than like that of giving effect to desire ; it would be a sort of necessity, following from the circumstances, and taking shape in your decision.   Or, to take another instance, suppose I am asked why I support or oppose the Poor Law Clauses of the Parish Councils Bill.   I *may* answer that I desire them, or am averse to them ; but the fundamental answer would seem to be : " Because they agree with, or are contrary to, all my ideas on the subject."   In the first case there is simply desire or aversion ; in the second there is the conception of a system of ideas working themselves out into a consistent whole.[1]

(ii.) *Is Pleasure the necessary object of Desire ?*— This brings us to the Psychology of Hedonism, and here we must note that the doctrine of Hedonism does not necessarily depend upon the old Psychology, which maintained that pleasure *is* the only thing desired.   It may be simply an opinion, serving as the basis of an ethical system, about the *value* of

[1] Cf. Mackenzie, p. 74.

Pleasure ; the opinion that it is *desirable*, not the demonstration that Pleasure is the exclusive object of desire. The latter view seems to depend upon a certain confusion between a present feeling of pleasure and the thought of future pleasure.[1] Both may determine action, but are not therefore the sole objects of Desire. To take a simple instance, the pleasure of satisfaction *presupposes* the desire of some definite object ; it cannot be achieved unless this object has first been desired. In thirst it is not Pleasure which is desired, but water, otherwise drinking could give no pleasure. When Pleasure *does* become the object of desire we have the voluptuary ; and he knows that he can only attain his object indirectly, by stimulating desires for definite things. Pleasure, we must remember, is an abstraction, and only to be found in the concrete complexity of mental life. Even *if* we go so far as to say that it is an aspect or element in everything we aim at, still that does not make it the *only* thing we aim at.

[1] Cf. Ward, *Ency. Brit.*, Ninth ed., vol. xx. pp. 74, 75.

G

LECTURE VIII

1. BEFORE passing from the theory of Volition it will be well to say something more about the connection of will with reflex action. The subject is one of those which lie on the border line of Psychology and Physiology, and besides being extremely interesting in itself it contributes a certain clearness to the whole modern view of the will.

The origin of the will out of simpler forms of action is discussed by James (pp. 92-101), by Ward (*l.c.* pp. 42, 43), and by Sully, (*Psychology*, p. 595 ; *Human Mind*, vol. ii. pp. 182, 192). The physiologist's view of the question may be found in the *Ency. Brit.*, article on "Physiology," Ninth ed., vol. xix. (pp. 28, 29); and Herbert Spencer, who has contributed much to the importance of the subject, deals with it in the chapters on reflex action and the will in vol. i. of his *Psychology*.

The general idea of reflex movement, or reflex action, seems to be that it is any movement started by what is called the incoming stimulus ; a stimulus, that is, entering by way of a nerve such as can carry what will be a sensation (an "afferent" nerve) up to the central nervous organs. In a more special or

strict sense it also means some rather definite movement corresponding mechanically to some rather
definite stimulus.   For instances we may begin with
the simplest kind, *i.e.* unconscious actions.   The
physiologists seem to be uncertain whether to regard
reflex movements as limited to those which have
psychological accompaniments—*i.e.* conscious movements, or as including unconscious movements ; and
Herbert Spencer, though he begins by including the
psychological accompaniment, often assumes that
the reflex movement is unconscious.   But we may
take as an instance of unconscious reflex movement
such a thing as the contraction of the pupil of the
eye when a light falls upon it ; we are conscious
of the light, but not of the contraction unless it is
specially pointed out.   The focussing of the lens of
the eye in looking at near or distant objects, and
the beating of the heart, with all the unconscious
functions carried on by the nervous system, are also
given as instances—although the beating of the heart
in its normal rhythm seems hardly to be regulated
(it is, of course, disturbed) by an incoming stimulus
from an afferent nerve.   The action of a carnivorous
plant in grasping its prey would seem to be a good
instance, but is excluded by physiologists on the
ground that reflex movement as they understand it
belongs only to organisms having a definite machinery
of action—a nervous system on the one hand, and a
muscular system on the other.

Next in the scale we have what are called sensori-
motor reflex movements ; movements, that is, in
which there is an impression of sense, and then
motion stimulated by that impression or sensation.
These are described as conscious, but involuntary or

semi-voluntary. Such are the closing of the eye when an object injurious to it approaches, the involuntary withdrawal of the hand from a hot or painful object, and the flow of tears when something gets into the eye.

With movements of this level we must compare certain very important movements which are not reflex in the stricter sense; these are *random* movements, such as we see in children, and *expressive* movements. Random movements may perhaps be reflex in the wider sense, but they are not definite movements co-ordinated to any purpose, or belonging to a definite stimulus; they are simply the sort of movement made by an infant when, *e.g.*, a bright light falls upon its eye. Expressive movements, such as the facial movements on tasting something sour, are of the same general kind.

In all these sensori-motor reflex actions we have the stimulus which is felt or perceived, but we have no idea of the movement to be executed before it has taken place; the idea comes only *after* the movement. On about the same *actual* level (not the same level of origin) we have again what are called the secondary reflex movements, or secondary automatic movements. The classical instance of these is that of the movements of the fingers of the skilled performer on the piano, movements which were once willed slowly and deliberately, but which have now become habitual or automatic. Our whole life is full of movements of this kind, all the co-ordinated movements made unconsciously by a grown-up person, which a child takes so long to learn to make. In these, as in the sensori-motor actions, there is no idea of the movement to be executed before it is carried out, although there is a stimulus which is felt or perceived.

Where, in all this, are we to look for the genesis of the will? in other words, for the beginning either of ideomotor action, or of action impelled by desire? It seems natural to look for it in the simplest form of reflex action, the unconscious movement which follows directly upon the unconscious stimulus, and this is the view apparently taken by Herbert Spencer. Ward, on the other hand, combats it, and there certainly are great difficulties in it, since our natural experience is all in the direction of voluntary action becoming reflex, not of reflex action becoming voluntary. Münsterberg, e.g., maintains very strongly that we have no experience at all of a simple reflex action becoming volitional, whereas we have abundant evidence of the reverse.

The two extreme views are, on the one hand that all movement is reflex (see James, p. 101), and on the other hand that all movements, even involuntary reflex actions, have been originally volitional. As between the two we may perhaps say that though the will *is* akin to reflex action in its more general meaning of an incoming stimulus which discharges itself in a movement, yet there are certain fixed reflex movements which do not tend to pass into volition. Instead, therefore, of looking for the origin of the will in the simplest of all reflex movements, such as the beating of the heart, we must (as Ward says) look for it in the random or expressive movements. These we may perhaps call *consequential*, meaning that they are the mere result of some stimulus, and have not been selected with a view to any purposive effect. But they are modifiable, and in them we soon get what we call subjective selection by help of ideas and feelings. That is, we get to know by experience what effect one of these movements will produce ; the stimulus brings up the idea, the idea brings up the action, and it comes under the head of what we have described as voluntary action.

Professor Bain has taken the view that the will originates from what he calls spontaneous action or discharges. Whether or not there are such spontaneous discharges seems matter of controversy ; but the tendency is to limit the number of such hypotheses, and we seem to meet all requirements by construing reflex action in the wider sense suggested ; that is, as including non-purposive action which has not become mechanical, and is capable of modification—random and expressive action.

2. *The higher and lower limits of morality.*—In order to have morality we must have the finite self; it is the finite self which distinguishes morality. In other words, the self must have begun to be aware of itself, and it must not yet have lost itself in knowing a higher self. When the higher limit is transcended, then morality is absorbed in a greater self.

(i.) About the lower limit Münsterberg has written an interesting work,[1] in which he takes an ultra-Kantian view. External conduct, he says, is no safe test of the existence of morality, and by judging from external conduct we have presupposed morality in the strict sense where it has not really existed. Individuals may, for instance, act so as to conduce to the good of the community, but that does not prove

[1] *Ursprung d. Sittlichheit.*

morality ; you must know from what motive they
act, and for the motive to be really moral he
demands that a rule should be obeyed for its own
sake, and in face of inclination. From this it
follows that the habit of moral action can only arise
by the association of rewards and punishments used
as training, by social discipline. Without this there
is no morality at all, for mere affection, or affectionate
regard for the good of the community, does not, on
his view, suffice to constitute morality.

Thus we have two questions arising :—

(*a*) Is Society *necessary* to the genesis of a moral
self ? (β) By what means does it, whether *necessary*
or not, aid this genesis ?

(*a*) We have already, in the lecture on Self-
consciousness, spoken of the first question : Is
Society necessary ? It seems to be conceivably
possible that the mere contrast of success and
failure within the individual might suffice to initiate
something like a moral judgment—the judgment of
approval, without a reflection of the self in society ;
and when we have got that, it can hardly be denied
that we have got something like a germ of the
moral consciousness.

(β) But then we have to ask in what way society
aids this genesis of the moral self. No doubt the
reflection of the self in the actions of other similar
bodies does much to promote the reflection of it in
the individual mind ; and, historically speaking, no
doubt the human individual does not originate in
isolation, but reflects some sort of community, so
that from the first the self goes beyond the bodily
unit. And without allowing that the consciousness
of a clash between personal inclination and the rule

is essential in all cases to moral action, or that society acts chiefly on the self by pains and pleasures, rewards and punishments, there is no doubt that the experience of approval and disapproval expressed by other selves will be a very effective way of drawing attention to *self*-approval or disapproval. It is this feeling of self-assertion, in which the self is approved of, which seems to constitute the essential element in the moral consciousness ; and this would begin practically with a society in which action was directed to the common welfare, for not only does such action constitute a great part of the self-assertion which meets with self-approbation, but that approbation is also intensified by its reflection in other minds.

In recognising the beginnings of moral conscious-ness wherever there is definite approval of the self on the ground of a relation to a common good (such as might arise from family or tribal affections), we make the lower limit of morality rather less definite than that drawn by Münsterberg. But his warning is a useful one, inasmuch as we do find in many accounts of animals what looks like self-sacrificing action for the benefit of others ; and unless we are prepared to admit these within the sphere of morality, we must insist on the presence of some idea of purpose or object by which the momentary self is tested and approved of, or the reverse.

(ii.) The question of the higher limit of morality hardly belongs to psychology, except in so far as morality hinges upon the consciousness of the self as a variable element. Where the religious consciousness emerges, and in so far as the religious attitude is maintained, the finite self is really

absorbed; and then the opposition or struggle characteristic of morality ceases to exist as a recognised
and fundamental opposition.

3. We have spoken of the self as the supreme
will and intelligence, and we have now to try how
far the idea of a willing self can be blended into a
whole with the intelligent self. Summarising the
view taken in the last lecture, we may regard the
self as an organised fabric, or organism, of which
the material is *ideas* taken in the widest sense and
carrying with them an accompaniment of feeling, *i.e.*
of immediate experience, including pleasure and
pain. If we examine what this self is, or what
there is in it, it seems to be really the whole world
as it is within the experience of the self—within, *i.e.*,
the single experience not merely as a train of
images in the mind, but as consisting of ideas
referred to reality. How can ideas, in this way
judged to be real, and taken as true, include purposes? We can understand that they should include
facts, but in what sense can they include *purposes?*
(i.) About facts as constituting the self, there is
not much more to be said. We have seen that the
search for an innermost self, a sacred holy of holies
in one's self which never changes and is never
obtruded upon, is hopeless. If we approach it in a
plain, practical way, we can draw no hard and fast
lines between elements in experience which belong
to the self, and those which do not. As James
points out, the loss of a man's friend, or house, or
profession, the loss of anything with which he is
identified, is undoubtedly a diminution of the self,
since it makes him other than he was, and less than

he was. In the same way, we must, to a certain extent, deem it true that a man's life consists in the abundance of the things which he possesses, as—for good or evil—they make him different.

(ii.) But if the self consists of those ideas of experience which are held to be facts, how can they include purposes, since an idea which represents a fact would seem to be without the ideal element, or element of difference from reality, which is required to make a purpose? How, that is, can such an idea suggest action? The answer would seem to be, because they are, or in so far as they are, only *conditionally* true. All our ideas are more or less selective ; they do not include the whole possible truth of reality, but only bits and extracts of it. Hence, speaking technically and strictly, *every* idea is referred to reality, not absolutely, but only conditionally ; in other words, certain reservations have to be made, apart from which it would not be really true. We may apply this to a real purpose, or a purpose that is at the same time a fact, in this way : your idea, say of the house in which you live, is your normal idea of it which goes on from day to day and week to week, as it *exists* and is *used ;* so if any accident happens to any part of it, if rain comes in at the roof, at once your permanent idea of the house differs from given reality ; the reality has got some-thing in it which your normal idea has not. Your idea can *then* only be true if it is conditional, and it would be expressed as "the house will be all right *when* the roof is mended"; that is to say, it will again conform to the normal and persistent idea of it, what it does for you and its use in your life. In the same way, the idea of a friend includes the rendering of service, and becomes conditional as soon as the necessity for service has arisen and not yet been met. We say " he will be just what I think him *if* he does so and so "; that is, our idea of him is for the moment discrepant from the actual reality ; there is something which the persistent idea requires which does not yet exist in the reality. It is thus that ideals are related to ideas in pure logic or pure psychology, and we may of course apply it to much larger subjects. We may say that, *e.g.*, the life of the people would be what it should be *if* so and so were done ; we assert something that, as it were, exists in reality but for an obstruction, but for some element in which reality deviates for the moment from our normal idea of what the reality *really* is, or means to be.

This view of the nature of ideals is important as requiring us—quite rightly—when we speak of an ideal, to state the actual reality upon which it is based, and the definite condition which separates our idea from the reality ; to state, that is, what it is which exists, and what we mean to do to bring it into harmony with its normal or persistent function or purpose. This has taken us somewhat beyond Psychology, but it illustrates what we have been trying to suggest, that the self which really exists is at once a moral and an intelligent self, a fabric of ideas accompanied with their affections of pleasure and pain, and having this tendency to assert themselves *in so far as* they become partly discrepant from reality.

We now have to approach the question whether this self, with its content of ideas and ideals, is exclusively and essentially social. Take for instance the idea of truth or of beauty; can we show that they are deducible without curtailment from the idea of the common or social good? The answer seems to turn on what we mean by social, and the best way to treat it will be to examine a certain form of what is meant by social, and then return to this contrast of social with non-social.

4. The relation of the social purpose to any other purpose is sometimes identified with that of altruism to egoism,[1] and we may examine this latter distinction first as a contrast to the view we have been taking. This is a distinction founded on our mere bodily separateness; I am the self connected with my body, and others are the selves connected with other bodies. On this view society becomes "self and others"; but, as Mr. Sidgwick has maintained, it is clear that from this point of view no one self can have prerogative over the others, so that in fact society comes to consist entirely of "others." This is purely psychological individualism, starting from the separate body as the separate self; and there are several ways in which we may attempt to arrive at morality based on such individualism.

(i.) We may hold with Professor Bain (*Emotions and Will*, p. 436 *sq.*) that, speaking generally, all will is selfish because it aims at a state of one's self; and that the character of a rational being is "to desire everything exactly according to its pleasure value."

(ii.) Or we may take what seems a more natural though perhaps less consistent view, and say that the natural will with which we start is egoistic,

[1] For a discussion of this see Mackenzie, *Manual of Ethics*, ch. 9.

looking at everything from the point of view of
its own particular interests; but that morality is
altruistic, and aims at the welfare of others. Reflection shows a man that from a generalised point
of view his own particular acts or purposes are of no
more importance than those of other people, and
thus we get to Bentham's rule, that one is to count
for one, and no one for more than one. For all
practical matters, including legislation, this is a good
sound rule.

(iii.) Again, we may follow Herbert Spencer and
" conciliate " egoism and altruism. It is obvious
that *de facto* either of them is a means to the other,
or that either of them requires the other as a means
to it; and so it would seem to matter little really
which we pursue, since to pursue it wisely we shall
have to pursue the other as well. This involves the
great practical truth that we cannot get our own
ends satisfactorily if we neglect other people, nor be
of much good to others if we neglect ourselves. But
can we get any further so long as we retain this
basis of self and others? The mere fact of their
being others does not seem to have any special kind
of purpose in it, nor the fact of a mere number of
persons to open up any moral end. It is parallel to
the logical question of the relation between connotation and denotation; we may try to distinguish the
denotation, but it is not really possible to think of
the individual thing with no connotation.

The real question must be, *what sort of thing is
it* that these others are? *what* is it that we want
the number of? Taking this as the governing consideration we may now leave the conception that
society consists of self and others, and try to get

at the thing from a different way of looking at the matter. The claim of society upon us does not seem to be founded on the fact that it is a plurality of bodily selves—or, if you like, of intelligences—but rather in the particular nature that their co-operation reveals ; and, psychologically speaking, it seems plain that we always act from the content of the self, which must consist of definite or positive ideas or ideals. It is not that other selves are merely instruments to the realisation of our ideals, but that we recognise the moral self to be the realisation of a certain nature which is the outcome of those selves working together in society. In other words, when we deal with other people, how-ever much we think we are being altruistic, our relation to them—of benevolence, justice, etc.—is founded upon some more positive point of view than that of mere otherness ; it is based, for instance, upon their humanity or citizenship, their capacity for education or for religion. We always consider what nature the individuals concerned are capable of developing, and this constitutes (*e.g.*) our standard in dealing with animals and children. We regulate our treatment of them in accordance with the *nature* or capabilities we find in them.

5. Having decided, then, to regard the self as a positive content to be realised, a certain set of ideas, let us now look at the system of ideas and ask whether—excluding the bad self—there are non-social elements in the legitimate moral self. We will take it as mere matter of fact, a question of the moral consciousness. It is clear, in the first place, that there is no intelligible principle by which

egoism equals the bad and altruism equals the good ;
but it might quite well be the case that all content
which can be systematised within the self is, as a
matter of fact, social. People with a profound faith
in all good things can always affirm that this is
so by bringing in " the long run." Is devotion to
metaphysics, *e.g.*, only justifiable on the ground of
the welfare of society? if so, it may be said, " No
doubt it is not immediately conducive to the welfare
of society, but 'in the long run' it will prove to be
so "—which is polite, if nothing else. But there are
more difficult cases than this. You may find a man
self-condemned before his own tribunal, because his
intellectual being is in disorder and he is not trying
to right it, as much as he would be if his social life
were in disorder. Must such a man prove that
systematising his intellectual being is conducive to
social welfare, before it is right for him to make
that his principal object in life? Must he show that
his intellectual completeness is a *social* ideal, and
can this be shown?

There is one way of disposing of this question
without throwing any light upon it, and that is by
widening the meaning of the "social self" to include
the harmonious adjustment and development of the
co-operative selves. In this way we may get in
whatever can be shown to be requisite to the entire
system of ideas, but it involves an evasion of the
question " Is it strictly social ? "

Another way of regarding it (which I prefer) is to
say that all the great contents of developed human
self—truth, beauty, religion, and social morality—
are all of them but modes of expression of the ideal
self. In any given social organisation the number

and nature of the entities composing it seem to a certain extent accidental and arbitrary; and clearly the given society or organisation is open to criticism. It is not ultimate, and we criticise it in respect of its power to find a complete harmony for the co-operating selves. It is interesting to note that in Plato's *Republic* the *ultimate* compass of life is the Good, Truth, and Beauty of the Universe; in other words, the greatest possibilities of human nature. It would be almost intolerable to have one's moral self given up to a little Greek community of ten or twenty thousand men, and to have all one's prospects depending upon the systematisation of one's will in accordance with the momentary end of that community; and accordingly Plato brings in this great doctrine of metaphysics, which has the effect of acting as a criticism. This is the final form of his ideal, and in it we have a certain grasp of something beyond the mere social organisation.

It may be suggested, therefore, that social duty —the duty which arises out of the relations of persons—is rather *one expression* of the universal self than its ultimate constitutive element; *i.e.* that the relations with a number of persons are *one* consequence of the nature of the self, one form of its universality.

6. Does this destroy self-sacrifice? If in getting rid of altruism we destroy the distinction between selfishness and self-sacrifice, there is, of course, a loss to moral philosophy. We must account for "unselfishness" in some way, and we may perhaps apply these terms to the different ways in which the systematisation of the self may be carried out, or again not carried out. Let us try four correlative terms :—

(i.) *Self-assertion* and *selfishness* as the good and bad terms of one order ; (ii.) *self-sacrifice* and *self-destruction* or *abandonment* as good and bad terms of the other order.

(i.) By *self-assertion* one would mean the attempt to be true to yourself in the fullest sense ; that is, to make as complete a system as possible of the ideas and purposes of the self. It would be the attempt at a certain kind of perfection ; not the individual perfection of the saint cut loose from the world, but a perfection including very likely work for others. *Selfishness* would be the same sort of thing caricatured. It would be an attempt at a kind of system, but narrowed rather than enlarged ; there would always be a certain indifference to the purposes in themselves, a tendency to take up a purpose or drop it according as it showed a tendency to private satisfaction or the reverse. But on the whole it would tend to an apparent removal of discord in the self, by narrowing instead of by enlarging.

(ii.) *Self-sacrifice*, again, as we actually find it, would mean the realisation, or attempt at realisation, of some special and important element which under the particular conditions is incompatible with the system and balance of the self as a whole. It would not include the whole content of the self, but would be the choice of what seemed all-important in a sense, and that again might perfectly well be some great work " for others." On the other hand it might just as well involve the abandonment of all work for others ; but it would still be self-sacrifice if it was a fair surrender of self—of the idea of perfection or completeness of the whole self-system—in order to realise something which seemed to be

H

supremely important. The complete antithesis of self-sacrifice is *self-destruction* or *self-abandonment*, where some wretched creature loses himself for something that does no good to any one, for some end that is thoroughly trivial, some freak or fancy. It differs from selfishness in that it is passionate, while selfishness is cool.

What we understand, then, by selfishness and self-sacrifice does not draw its meaning from the antithesis of self and others, but from the different ways of using the contents which constitute our self, and all of which practically extend beyond our mere bodily self. Even in the search for private pleasure we use contents that go beyond the bodily self, since we are obliged to act for the welfare of others ; so that even in the pursuit of mere pleasure we get beyond the distinction of egoism and altruism.

LECTURE IX

REASONABLE ACTION

THE difficult question of "reasonable action," as the phrase goes, receives considerable attention in Mr. Sidgwick's *Method of Ethics*, and he has also written an interesting article in *Mind* (N. S. vol. ii. No. 6) on "Unreasonable Action." We will consider some of the difficulties which have to be met.

1. Taking first the psychological meaning of the phrase, we get something of a contradiction. The earliest distinct meaning of the term "to reason" is that of computation or calculation. Our word "reason" corresponds with the Latin *ratio* and the Greek λόγος, and in its simplest sense that means what we call ratio, or sometimes proportion. Reason in this sense, then, means the putting together of ratios, or the comparison of numerical relations in one sense or another, in order to elicit the conclusion, the result or answer.

In very early language, as we have pointed out, there were words indicating knowledge which seem capable of being applied to almost any content of the mind ; the attempt to distinguish accurately, *e.g.* to distinguish "reason," came later. One of the

most definite, and at the same time most difficult, of
these early meanings is this of computation or calculation.   We find it, *e.g.*, in Plato, and there is
evidence of it in the relation of the words "ratio"
and "reason."   In a slightly enlarged sense we may
take it as the intellectual perception of relations.[1]
But how can it, in this sense, either mark a distinction between desirable and undesirable objects of
action ; or, on the other hand, be in itself an impulse
to action ?   Taking as the simplest type of this
kind of reason the judgment "two and two make
four," it is not clear how it can be connected with,
or influence, the impulses to action.

There is a famous saying of Aristotle that "intelligence by itself is not a motive power," in which
the term used for intelligence is that which Plato
applies to the mathematical reason, the perception
of relations.   It expresses the difficulty that at first
sight the idea of reasonable action is a contradiction.
We cannot see how the two terms hang together,
nor what is meant by calling an action reasonable.
For instance, does the fact that more calculation is
involved in the framing of any idea make it a more
reasonable object of moral action ?

2. Passing on from this elementary meaning, we
may consider a few explanations of the term.

(*a*) *Means known.*—One way is to say that action
becomes reasonable when the means to a given end
are properly calculated.   The great typical theory
which reduces moral reasonableness to this is that
of Hedonism, according to which the end is fixed
and constant (the amount of pleasure), and moral

[1] Cf. Hobbes's *Computation or Logic.*

deliberation is the calculation of means to attain that
end. The same meaning can be ascribed, whatever
the end, provided that the end is assumed to be
given ; and thus we might explain "reasonable
action " to mean " action calculated so as to be suitable to the accepted end." This does not necessarily
involve the admission that amount of pleasure is the
sole and universal end of action ; but there is still
the difficulty that mere conduciveness to a given end
does not seem to express the full sense in which we
use the words " reasonable action," for, as Sidgwick
is constantly insisting, they come to mean almost
the same as *right* action.

There is one way of explaining the ordinary
usage which may carry us a little further. If we
take as the end something very abstract, such as
goodness, perfection, or happiness, then its concrete
realisation is really made what it is by the means
we adopt to it. If, *e.g.*, you say your object is to be
good and to live a good life, then I ask you what
you mean by a good life ; and the concrete way of
living which you point out as a means to good life
in your sense really qualifies the whole thing, and is
the first distinct statement which gives me a definite
idea of what you mean by good life. When the
end is very abstract, then the *means*, taken in a
wider sense, is really the beginning of definiteness ;
so that even when we start from the simple idea of calculating the means to a given end, we find the *reason-
ing* will affect our concrete notion of the end itself.

Here we get a point of ethical—perhaps also of
psychological—interest. The means which we adopt
to any purpose are, ethically speaking, much the
same as consequences. They are something that

has to be taken into the bargain, *the price we pay* for the action ; and we cannot really know what is the cost of the purpose as a whole until we know what means we are prepared to take in order to carry it out. Until we see how the whole thing looks, as set out in that way, we do not know what the ethical cost really is, and how it is morally related to our scheme of life. Here, then, we get beyond the mere calculation of the means to the end, and a further meaning is suggested.

(β) *End fully and clearly conceived.*—Reasonable action may perhaps mean that the end of our action is clearly and completely conceived, is set before us in all its causes and all its effects. Such action is deliberative as opposed to impulsive, and we should certainly be apt to say that a man is acting reasonably when he acts deliberately, with full consideration of the means to what he wants to bring about and of the consequences of what he wants to bring about. On the other hand, the object or purpose, though quite plainly and completely conceived, *may* be unreasonable in the general sense we are now considering. If, *e.g.*, you deliberately set yourself to overreach another person, to get more than your share, you might quite naturally be said to be an unreasonable man, to be acting unreasonably. Or if, again, a judge has decided against me in the discharge of his duty, I should be said to act unreasonably if I tried, however deliberately, to revenge myself on him.

We may get this kind of unreasonableness either from passion or ignorance ; probably in all cases there is a certain amount of ignorance involved, and so far we may say the action is not clearly and

completely conceived. But leaving out the great
moral purposes of life—*i.e.* not saying that indifference to them constitutes intellectual ignorance—we
know that there are people who pursue quite relent-
lessly a bad or selfish purpose, which is conceived
with perfect clearness ; and even these would probably be said to be acting unreasonably. Apart
from these it is probable that most revengeful
people, the people with a grievance, have a good
deal of intellectual darkness in their minds as well
as of passion ; they are generally imbued with what
we may call fictitious motives.

(γ) *Reasonable, then, may = fair, impartial.*—We
find a further contrast for reasonable action in
this fact, that a man who is quite deliberate and
clear in his ideas may yet be pronounced unreasonable, unfair, unjust, selfish, partial, prejudiced by
passion, because he is trying to overreach some one.
This brings us nearer to the sense in which we
commonly use the word unreasonable in moral
matters. It means that in some way a man has
let his passion have too free a sway ; or that he
claims too much to himself; and in opposition to
this, reasonable action would be described by such
words as impartial, unbiassed, disinterested.

(δ) *Reason v. Feeling.*—Under this head we get
two meanings for "reasonable action." (i.) It may
imply the collision between Reason and Feeling,
and then unreasonable means self-indulgent, self-
absorbed, letting personal desires get the mastery.
We constantly think of Reason as opposed to Desire,
and in this sense we think of it rather as negative
than positive ; we must all tend to feel that to the
commonplace moralist the function of the Reason is

to point out to us from day to day what *not* to do.
Plato, in his *Republic*, when he is describing the
two elements in the will of man, says that there is
the appetite making you desire to drink, and something else which prevents you, and that something
else is finally the Reason (which he is speaking of
as the "calculating" faculty). This becomes intelligible only in connection with the positive content
of the Reason, which we shall try to exhibit in its
true character; and this appears in the *Republic* in
the sixth and seventh books. But in all common
life and commonplace morality the positive character
and content of the Reason is apt to be left in the
background. Reason appears chiefly as something
which commands, and commands by way of pro-
hibition ; it checks and "inhibits," as the physiologists
say. We cannot accept the suggestion that the
mark of reasonable action is either the absence of
Feeling or opposition to Feeling. (Kant had, at
one period, some idea of this kind, and within recent
years it has been revived by Münsterberg.[1]) It is
quite true, as we have seen, that action may start
through pure ideas, without desire, but on the other
hand it does not follow that ideomotor action is
reasonable action. There is ideomotor action in the
case of a man who is practically a monomaniac, and
in whom a dominant idea upsets his normal ideas.

(ii.) *Obedience to a Maxim or Truism.*—We get
the second form of this idea of reasonableness in the
suggestion that it may consist in obedience to this
or that abstract maxim which approves itself to the
intellect by a sort of simplicity. It seems natural
to us, *a priori* as people say, convincing in some

[1] *Ursprung d. Sittlichheit*, p. 27.

form. The English philosopher Clarke thought
that we could somehow account for reasonableness
of action by comparing the conceptions of moral
relations to the perception of intellectual relations ;
that in some way we can *see* the rightness of moral
relations as we see that two and two make four, or
as we see the more beautiful and complex relations
in higher mathematical ideas. But he also formulates
two moral laws which seem to be taken as certain
because they are so simple that they commend
themselves as truisms to the intellect. Sidgwick
approves these laws, and it would perhaps be fair to
say that what positive doctrine there is in *Methods
of Ethics* is equivalent to them.[1] They are called
the laws of Equity and Benevolence, and they are
derived from the principle we have already dealt
with, that we must, theoretically, suppose one person
to be as good or as important as another, if there
is no reason for making any difference between
them.

The Law of Benevolence runs : "What I
account reasonable for me to do for myself, I
account equally reasonable for me to do for others."
In plain English : "What is good for me is good
for others." And the Law of Equity is just the
converse : "What it is reasonable in other people
to do for me, it is also reasonable that I should do
for them." Of course, as Sidgwick points out, these
axioms involve an assumption, which they merely
apply ; the assumption that there is something that
is "reasonable" for me to do for myself.

Given this assumption that there is something
"reasonable" for me, then the axiom that it is equally

---

[1] Cf. *Methods of Ethics*, pp. 360 *sq.*

reasonable for others is natural enough ; it finds a common expression in the proverb, " What is sauce for the goose is sauce for the gander." Assuming that A's happiness is worth seeking, then B's happiness is worth seeking also in so far as it is not different from A's ; *i.e.* in so far as B corresponds to the general type of A. The real value of the axioms lies in the qualities taken as the base of their application. By taking the distinctively human qualities we get a wide humanitarian principle ; if we were to include the accidents of birth or learning, rank or position, we should not get the same result.

The abstract idea of " reasonable," then, really indicates that there must be a concrete purpose to which the term moral reasonableness, strictly speaking, applies. The claim is relative to particular standards, and we are in the habit of assuming for general purposes a sort of general average standard ; in this way we get the idea that the reasonable is mediocre, the average, or the "golden mean." We get, in fact, a *negative* idea of it, to which is due the remarkable and somewhat melancholy fact that when we call upon people to " be reasonable," we are generally urging them *not* to do something. When we urge any one to do something arduous, to break through a commonplace tendency, to make a generous exertion, we do not say " Do be reasonable " ; but rather when we want him to come down to some sort of average standard.

But this negative or abstract idea, so far as it is right, can only rest on a positive or concrete idea. As stated in these simple truisms, the " reasonable " seems to be just a very brief and unimportant outline abstracted out of a real organised purpose of life.

It is from the great practical purposes of life that it must be derived.

This brings us to the final suggestion. Reasonable action is not (*a*) opposed to ignorance of means chiefly, nor yet (*β*) to ignorance of the end chiefly. Nor is it opposed chiefly (*γ*) to the unjust, nor (*δ*) to action impelled by feeling, or contradicting one of the obvious truisms of general application. Yet it has a certain relation to all of this, and may be summed up as *action directed to a positive object having the character of rationality*.

(*ε*) Reasonableness as a quality of a concrete purpose, then, is the final suggestion. We have seen that the view of Reason as calculation suggests a positive end ; that what we took to be a simple isolated purpose becomes, when we have calculated and estimated all the means and all the consequences, no longer an isolated object, but a scheme of life. In a similar way an abstract axiom or truism demands explanation and filling in ; it appears that what is satisfactory for A would not be suitable for B, and thus the positive nature of A and B has to be taken into consideration.

And so we arrive at the notion of a systematic purpose in life, in which the contents of the self can be organised. Such a purpose, if it is rational, must have the two great characteristics of *self-consistency* and *consistency with the whole of experience ;* that is, as we said in the last lecture, it must be so far one with reality that the conditions distinguishing it from the actual reality are assignable and can be explained, while they also point in the direction of a more harmonious reality. It is very important to a true ideal or purpose that it should be understood as the *whole* systematised self or experience, not merely the unreal element.   Our ideal of society, *e.g.*, is not confined to the future, nor to the points at which our opinions become discrepant from reality ; it is the normal view of social facts, past, present, and future, as we understand them.   The unrealised element is a mere rounding off, or completion of the whole.   A certain modification from the actual fact may be necessary to a practical ideal, but it is all, so to say, in one piece ; we have not a given fact on one side, and an idea of something future on the other.   The discrepancy in your ideal from reality depends for justification on your right understanding of the given fact as it is.   It is a mistake, therefore, to say that the ideal is confined to the future.   Just as Natural Science has to do with what happened in the past or at any time, so a right moral ideal has to do with giving true value to elements in the past or present.

To understand how this really applies to Psychology, we may consider what is involved in an analysis of life.   Professor Bonamy Price, when analysing the working processes of a great London bank, spoke of laying it on the dissection table ; and our procedure should be something like this when we are considering what human lives are really like. For instance, we may analyse a moral life with a view of bringing out its parallelism with the theoretical structure of the intelligence ; and we may consider how its purposes are combined together, and co-ordinated with each other or subordinated to some one purpose, noting how the system fails in some parts and is more systematically combined in others. And we may ask how the object of the will can be said to have the characteristic of rationality, and find that, as with other organic structures, it lies in its capability of evading discord, of receiving new experience without creating discord.[1]

3. There are two final characteristics of moral action to be noted ; *i.e.* Effort and Self-judgment. How far are these essential to moral action ?

Effort.—(i.) Professor James deals with effort in the *Text-book*, pp. 443 *sq.* He calls attention to the fact that the sensual man never ventures to speak of his conduct as a victory over his ideals, whereas a man who has made an effort to do right speaks of a victory over his passions. Common language recognises effort in the one case and yielding in the other. This effort, James says, is the effort of attention to an idea, and he illustrates it by the elementary case of keeping the right name of the action proposed before the mind. If the man who was tempted to drink, instead of saying " this is to keep me warm," or calling it " hospitality," were to keep before his mind that it is " drinking," it would be moral effort.[2]

It is perhaps a fair description of effort, then, to say that it is the process by which an idea establishes itself which has to call for numerous reinforcements. On the whole, and generally speaking, the *temptation* is *given ;* it is intense in its character, and because it is a temptation to something unworthy it is partial and narrow. On the other hand the right, the idea which is good, has to conquer by going through a

[1] Cf. James, *Text-book of Psychology*, p. 430. We have to bear in mind that the mere fact of an action being initiated by ideas does not prove its reasonableness. It is the nature of ideas which matters.

[2] Cf. also Sidgwick in *Mind*, *loc. cit.*, where he enlarges upon the effects of self-deception.

process. It has to call up reinforcements through all the various complicated relations of the content of the self, and this may partly explain why we speak of effort when we do right and of yielding when we do wrong. It is difficult to reverse the application of the terms, because the right will always be connected with the larger purpose ; but in certain complicated states of mind something like it may occur. If, *e.g.*, a lawful and intense affection (say filial affection) is competing with an attractive and not very creditable scheme of life (say some ambition), then there may be present the peculiar sense of effort, of the idea reinforcing itself in trying to do wrong, and a sense of yielding in giving way to the right and natural affection.[1] (See also Sully's *Human Mind*, ii. 288.)

Is the sense of Effort necessary to Morality ?— We may perhaps say that the form of effort is in some degree a *sine qua non*, because the wider purpose in asserting itself will always demand a certain " reinforcement." But that is one side of the truth only, and morality is not to be judged by the intensity of the sense of effort. The will is real, and realised, in habits and institutions ; and the sense of self-affirmation which arises from the agreement of the will with its outer and realised self, is one of the most important factors in the guidance of the moral will. If all morality were effort, we should be in an unhappy state where there was no realisation and no sense of affirmation in the existing social world. Those people who think it their duty to be always in a state of moral excitement, fighting against

---

[1] Of course there is a still wider purpose in alliance with the natural affection, but the latter may be the most prominent.

themselves with an intense and arduous moral effort, are probably wrong. If not, the formation of good habits would be sheer waste ; but the formation of good habits is an important factor in the realisation of the wider purposes. It is rather the width of the effort after right, and its *bona fides*, not the *feeling of its intensity*, which is the essential point in the moral state.

(ii.) Finally, we have to say a few words on the nature and necessity of moral self-judgment.

(*a*) There is one kind of moral judgment of which the predicate is a positive idea of a course of action, and the subject is " What I ought to do." Here we have a real perception or inference. It is concrete, it applies to the circumstances of the moment, and it is constructive ; that is, it depends on successfully understanding how what is actually *given* may be made to conform to its idea. To suppose that the moral choice is always between two ready-made courses is a great mistake ; we are like scientific men with new facts before them, and our duty is to be equal to the situation. *This* judgment is essential to morality and is the very process of morality.

(*β*) A second kind of moral judgment is one of which the predicate is " good " or " bad," and the subject an act or person. " A. B. is good (or bad)." " That action was good (or bad)." The very words good and bad are an embodiment of this moral judgment, and show that it is used ; but yet we have the current prohibitions, " Judge not," " Don't impute motives." We are urged to judge the act and not the agent, but we cannot really separate the act from the moral agent. What we probably do in commonplace moral judgment is to refer the act by its common accepted name to a sort of fictitious unreal agent; we assume a sort of normal, average person, and so get a working morality. "Stealing is wrong," *i.e.* normally, for a normal agent. In such a judgment we do not take into account the individual circumstances of any actual moral case; we are judging abstractly, hypothetically, assigning the act to an assumed agent.

To get deeper we must judge the motive, and the motive may be described as that part of the action which attracted the agent *at the price of* the means and foreseen consequences. We must not leave out these, but must apply to the agent the fact that the motive was able to attract him at the price of its consequences; and an object attractive in this way is an embodiment of character. If we knew it fully —which we never could—we could judge categorically of the character displayed in the act. As it is, we judge hypothetically of the motive; we say, "*If* it was as it seems to be, *then* it was a bad action," but we do not profess to know what is the state of the individual character.

Also, we do pass moral judgments on people. We class them as good or bad with a pretence of categorical judgment, *i.e.* judgment without an "*if.*" This is really a judgment relative to our current standpoint, and seems to be based on a general impression of the limits of a man's character as compared with his opportunities. If such a judgment were complete, and based on the knowledge it really requires, it would be categorical; but then it would pass beyond mere morality. All we can do is to try roughly to understand how much a man had given to him, and what he did with it; where he started, and how far he got. Then we have to make allowances for what we don't know, and we find ultimately that we cannot pass any categorical judgment at all ; we do not know the conditions with sufficient accuracy to say he was " good " or " bad."

All general moral judgment, then, except the judgment on things to be done, is hypothetical, and useful only as a sort of first approximation to actual circumstances. We do not venture to say that every one who steals is a bad man ; but we do say that there are strong presumptions against him, and it is useful to have a current sense or judgment of the kind, to keep us straight. But the only really categorical, concrete, moral judgment is that which determines what the course of action is, by adopting which we can be equal to the occasion ; and the predicate of this judgment is a course of action, and not a moral term of approval or reproach.

Finally, that which constitutes the measure of morality seems to be the actual identification of the private self with the universal self, the actual surrender of the will to the greater will of the system to which we belong. We cannot judge by the *feeling* of being good or bad ; that is absolutely deceptive. The best people often have a feeling of being bad, and Emerson writes of a lady who told him that "the sense of being perfectly dressed affects the mind with an inward comfort which religion is unable to bestow." Effort and judgment, again, though implied in morality, are not measures of it ; they are only indispensable conditions.

LECTURE X

BODY AND SOUL

1. THE general problem of the relation between Body and Soul has been an interesting case of progressive analysis. It begins with the simple view of the phenomena which precludes mechanical explanation, and may be called the magical view ; and then by an analysis, which seems very modest, we are driven back into explaining part after part of this series of phenomena into mechanical action, or some sort of regular intelligible action. And when finally the magical element has been driven back into a dark corner, we ask ourselves whether the spiritual or profound principle for which we are searching, the larger view of phenomena, may not really apply to the whole of them taken as a system, and not, by preference, to the unexplained or mysterious element. The suggestion arises that *mystery* is not essential to a spiritual view of things, and that what is *more* or *higher* is so from some kind of value attaching to its arrangement in a system.

We will begin our study of the problem by a general sketch of the stages we have personally gone through in our education (*not* of the history of philosophy). Probably most of us have at one time

thought that *mind* is a *thing*, which thinks and seems
to move the body—with which it is co-extensive—
without any assignable mechanism.   As we begin to
be educated we find out, *e.g.*, that the mind is not
present at the tips of the fingers where we seem to
feel ; that the actual skin and flesh is not sensitive,
but only the nerve, upon pressure of which feeling
follows.   A further stage of the same discovery is
when we learn that if a nerve is cut anywhere
between finger and brain there will not be any
sensation in the finger ; so that really the feeling at
the finger tips is, to a certain extent, not a mistake,
but an illusion.   It is analogous, as Lotze says,
to the sort of effect we may get by feeling a
thing with a walking-stick ; we seem to feel at the
other end of the stick that it is smooth, or soft, or
gritty.   Aristotle was aware of this, though he did
not know that the nerves were the means of sensation ;
he knew that we could feel through a film round the
flesh very much as if the sensitive part itself was
touched.

Then we must all remember when we found out
—what Mill points out—that the will is not magical,
that, *e.g.*, a numbed arm will not move.   That is, the
sequence of movement upon will is not infallible, is
not magical, but depends upon a certain mechanism
which may go wrong ; we do not know whether it
will really act except by trying.   Experience of this
kind, however we come by it, whether by observation,
or reading, or hearsay, makes us withdraw the
magical notion of the will from the outlying parts of
the body ; until, in popular culture, we get a sort of
idea of the soul as a little creature sitting in the
brain.   As Lotze suggests, we think of it as like a

player on a keyed instrument receiving telephonic messages from the nerves into the central organs of the brain, and sending down motor messages in return. This is the modern development of Descartes's idea that the soul resides in the pineal gland, the only portion of the brain that happens not to be doubled.

This idea of Lotze's, then, is really the up-to-date form of the commonplace distinction of Soul and Body as two things, as we shape it by our popular culture and knowledge of physiology. Though magic has given way to the idea of mechanism so far as the *body* is concerned, still in the great popular view the soul remains as a magical source of action, a substance or thing which is not the body, and which acts upon the body. We find a similar view in the less profound parts of Plato, those parts where he is inclined to regard the soul as a separate creature, acting upon the body and surviving it (though he probably did not even know that the work of thought goes on by means of the brain).

We may indicate what is technically important in such a view as follows, using Greek letters to denote states of consciousness, or psychological events, and English letters to denote states of body, or physical and material events. According to it we get a series, say of action following upon an incoming stimulus, like A, β, C ; in which A is the shock transmitted by a mechanical state of the body, β the pure soul state *without any state of the body corresponding to it*, and C the state of the body involved in the motor impulse sent out.

Then analysis pushes further to a point hardly reached until we study psychology. The change of

bodily states from A to C is alleged to be continuous, and though we can neither prove nor
disprove it, there is no reason to doubt that it is
so. So we get the series A, B, C, where A is the
incoming shock, B the state of the central organs,
and C the motor impulse. But if A and B are
enough to account for C, what need is there for
the soul? Even though we grant that A, B, C is
accompanied by α, β, γ, that is quite different from
saying that the true course of sequence is A β C.

Lotze is very interesting on this point, just
because he is making the transition himself. He
cannot quite abandon the idea of a soul-thing, acting
out of itself, but he is prepared to admit that action
of the soul is excited by some change in the bodily
state. When we have got as far as this, when we
have a continuous system of bodily changes without
any interruption from psychical changes, we have
got rid of the magical in principle. The soul ceases
to be a series of inexplicable reactions, and we come
back to the conception of Plato and Aristotle at
their best—the conception that the spiritual view
is that which regards experience as a mechanically
intelligible whole.

2. (i.) *Things interacting.*—Taking this more in
detail, we get first the possible view of Body and
Soul as two things interacting; the view we have
been describing. It is the view which we naturally
take when we first begin to reflect, and seem to feel
the soul as a state of mind which moves the body;
and we find it in the common language even of
philosophers. In James's *Text-book* (p. 5) he says
that all *mental* states are followed by *bodily* activity

of some sort ; and Granger in his *Psychology* (p. 15) insists that a state of *mind* may be excited by a state of body. If we take this view seriously, we get—as we have seen—the sequence A, β, C, in which A is physical, β psychical, C physical ; and many difficult questions arise, such as whether the seat of the soul in the body is apart from the nervous system, or whether " the soul " can exercise mechanical force, or how it affects the nervous centres.   Lotze discusses these questions, and Bradley considers them fair questions for discussion. Hegel, on the other hand, rejects them as meaning-less ; for him the soul cannot be thus separated from the body and considered as acting upon it.

We may at any rate get rid of the elementary difficulty by rejecting the formula A, β, C.   No psychologist will seriously maintain it, for it ex-presses the confusion of psychological and physio-logical consequence.   In other words, it expresses the view that the soul is separated from the body, and is acting upon it from the outside.

Our formula, then, must be in one sense or another the two series running side by side, A, B, C, α, β, γ ; and the question before us is, how to interpret them.

(ii.) *Bare Concomitance.*—The first and simplest explanation of, or way of looking at, the two series, is that of bare concomitance ; the suggestion, that is, that they accompany each other, but that we can say no more about their relation ; that they run on side by side, neither affecting the other.   The view is an interesting one, but not really an explanation at all ; it simply says that we must treat the two series as disconnected, because we do not know how to connect them. And in psychology no doubt we are obliged to treat the mental series as on the whole complete in itself; we must try to show that in some sense it hangs together, without being explained by states of brain, and so on.

If we do try for an explanation we are forced to one of two extremes. We must either say that Soul and Body are really independent, and Will a sort of junction between them, so giving up all chance of explanation; or we must say that they are *aspects* or *manifestations* of the same underlying unity. But an explanation that is not more definite than this is really no explanation at all; it is simply a rule of method that for the present we are unable to say anything about the connection, and that we must therefore treat each series as if it were disconnected.

(iii.) But it is difficult to repose in an attitude like that. Man naturally presses on to some explanation, and so we get the next theory, the theory that the soul is an effect and not a cause. The results of such a theory are somewhat repellent, but it is becoming dominant, and must be faced. Briefly stated it is, that the course of mental events has no causative influence of its own at all, but is *a series of separate effects produced by the accompanying physical events.*

If either series is to be the effect of the other it seems clear it must be the mental series, if only because the bodily series seems to be continuous while the mental series does not. Then, taking this view of consciousness as a mere accompaniment of bodily events, let us look again at our series A, B, C, *a*, *β*, *γ*. A, a state of the body, is now the cause of

B, another state of the body, and also of a, its accompanying mental event; B again is the cause of C, and of β. On the other hand, a is not the cause of β, and has no connection with it; β is not the cause of γ, and much less is a the cause of A, or β in any sense the cause of B. The series of consciousness has no effect on the bodily series.

This is the view with which modern psychology is coquetting, and for many reasons it is difficult to take another; but if frankly stated and worked out it carries us a long way. For instance, in this view pleasure and pain, considered as feelings, would have no effect whatever on actions; they could not, as part of the mental series. Indeed, as a somewhat rash writer has amusingly said, it would appear as if the whole of life might go on the same if consciousness were not present, the determining feature being natural selection.[1] The organism would be a machine which would produce those movements necessary for the preservation of the race, and consciousness would make no difference. A clear instance of this extreme theory is Münsterberg's view that, except in certain complicated instances, my idea of the movement I am about to make is not in any degree a cause of that movement. A certain stimulus calls up a movement because natural selection has picked it out as desirable; and the idea is prior, only because less time intervenes between the stimulus and the idea which it suggests, than between the stimulus and that perception of the movement which is subsequent to its being carried out. Thus the whole conception of our previous idea of the movement being the cause

[1] Fawcett, *Riddle of the Universe.*

would be an illusion ; and even in the complicated cases where Münsterberg admits a certain influence, it is only the bodily side of the idea which has that influence.

Of course this view rests to a great extent on the assumption of the conservation of energy, or the persistence of force, the assumption on which we conduct physical science in the present day. In the physical series, A, B, C, the circuit of mechanical motion is complete, and there seems to be no room for any generation of movement outside it, or any loss inside. Nothing but motion, according to the ordinary idea, can be the equivalent of energy ; and the assumption is that the energy is all accounted for by this continuous cycle of movements, the one of which excites the other in a never-ending series.

The very clearness of this view leads to certain difficulties.[1]   The series a, β, γ, are represented as (i.) effects, or at least events, having no causes ; for the mechanical cause A is on this hypothesis fully accounted for in the mechanical effect B, so that no causal action remains to account for a and β ; and (ii.) causes, or at least events, without effects. This is obvious from the statement, and both are difficult to believe.

And finally there is one more point, upon which we would not lay too much stress. Of course the bodily states, as well as the mental states, are all of them objects of experience, of perceiving ; and more particularly our whole idea of nature as a system of mechanical causes is only an abstraction out of the whole of our knowledge. In short, we

[1] See Bradley, *Appearance and Reality*, p. 327.

have to take into consideration the effects of subjective idealism.   But this argument does not help
us in detail, for this reason.   If we have once undertaken the task of classifying our experience, and
arranging the parts in a reasonable system according
to their nature, we have no right at every moment
to say, " After all it is only my own experience, only
an ideal construction." Such an attitude does not
enable us to change the nature of the facts from
what they present themselves as being in our experience ; it only prevents us in general from thinking that the mechanical system of nature (*e.g.* as a
system of atoms) is an ultimate fact.

(iv.) Another view which may be suggested is
that which speaks of the soul as an *ideal aspect of the
body*, or the *ideality* of the body ; and this seems to
contain an attempt in the right direction.   The only
way of avoiding the difficulty of making consciousness entirely an effect, is to refuse to make the
abstraction between the bodily and the mental series.
In philosophy it is generally an abstraction of some
kind that leads us to ultimate difficulties ; we
separate two things, set them over against each
other, and then try to reduce each of them to the
other, and this is perhaps what we have been trying
to do here.   The mental fact does not exist by
itself, and it is not proved that it can ; and though
from the point of view of the onlooker bodily facts
do seem to exist without mental facts, yet the law
of causation forbids us to admit that they are the
same when they exist separately as when accompanied by mental facts.   This cuts both ways.   It
may be said to show that mind depends upon the
existence of body, and so far as our experience goes,

and under present conditions, it does seem to show something of the sort. But on the other hand it shows that we need not raise the question whether pure thought, or pure feeling, can work upon the body, for within our experience there is no pure thought or pure feeling—*i.e.* no thought or feeling which is devoid of a physical accompaniment. Mental effect is both bodily and mental, and the moment we split it up into a bodily and mental series—except for the convenience of our science— we get away from the facts. Thus it is quite possible that an idea, or a feeling of pleasantness, may cause a movement of the body through its corresponding bodily state, and then theorists of the the one side or the other may say, " But the bodily state is only an accident of the mental event," or " the mental is only an accident of the bodily event." To this we reply : " How do you know this ? " All that we know is that the thing is given as one with two sides, and there is no reason to make difficulties by an abstraction which does not heed the facts. We may find another instance of the factitious difficulty in the conceptions of contiguity and similarity, when the question is asked whether con- tiguity is a bodily or mental principle. Or, again, in the question whether a theory of pleasure and pain deals with a bodily or mental principle. We must refuse to make the abstraction, and then the question falls to the ground. No doubt the bad form of the doctrine of association has been largely generated by the attempt to make it merely a bodily principle ; the object being to enable us to regard the mind as something like a rack full of photographs, out of which one is taken when a particular image recurs.

And it is convenient to say with James and others that the paths of association are the paths of the brain, as possibly they are. But after all the machinery is unknown to us ; the psychical combination is what we know, and we must simply examine the psychical action and assume that the machinery of the body is in some way adapted to carry out the psychical modes of combination.

Then it is natural to ask what is added by the view that the soul is the ideality of the body, to the view which simply accepts two aspects, two concurrent series ? The answer is, that it calls attention to the individual organised nature of the soul. When we are told about a bodily series of events accompanied by a mental series, we tend to feel as if the soul had been broken up into a set of detached incidents, without combination. We have to remember that after all, the soul, the contents of the soul as we know it, form an individual system full of character and personality ; that it is quite as characteristically individual and belonging to itself as the body is, and certainly at a higher level ; and that while its constituent elements include of course the qualities of the body, they include also a whole world of other qualities and relations. Thus we get quite a different estimate of the importance of the soul if we regard it from this point of view, from what we do if we allow ourselves to regard it as simply a set of events accompanying certain changes of the body. The question of *value* is really distinct from that of the nature of the causal connection between mind and body ; and it is difficult to see why some of our best writers are so sensitive to admitting that, from a historical standpoint, the soul or mind is conditioned

by the causation or machinery of the sequence of
bodily states. The important point is, what the
thing actually *is ; i.e.* what is its nature, and in what
does its organisation consist. We are quite accustomed to find that the things we value most have
been able to develop through a system of mechanical
causation.

The only theoretical difficulty that threatens the
spiritual character of our world arises when we
separate the two elements, body and soul, and then
try to reduce either of the unrealities to the other.
If we think that because the soul is conditional upon
the processes of a bodily organism, therefore it is
nothing more than the processes of bodily organisation, then we have made for ourselves an unnecessary
and serious difficulty. In a work of art we know
that it is mechanically conditioned in every part, but
we do not think that makes any difference to its
value ; in other words, we suppose that the causes
which gave it value are capable of expressing themselves through the mechanical processes which produce
the work. And in the same way we have to suppose,
not that the spiritual element begins at a given point
in nature, but that the whole process of nature is
capable of being instrumental to the development of
that which is of spiritual value.

(v.) There are two great subjects which we shall be
expected to mention, but on which there is little to
say in this connection. The first, the question of
Free-will, does not really arise at all. No one maintains that we ourselves made our positive qualities.
Our language, our ancestors, our religion, our leading
ideas, the country we live in, are given to us, not
made by us. But the machinery by which life is

carried on does not affect our free-will at all, except
of course in so far as it limits or determines our
power of being influenced by similar experience to
other people's.   In the sense that we all have
positive advantages and disadvantages, for which we
cannot account, as compared with other people, no
doubt our *relative* freedom and capacity is determined.
But admitting that each of us is a positive system,
with certain definite qualities which he did not himself
create, then the mere mode in which the machinery
of the organic system determines those positive
qualities is of no possible importance, and cannot
affect any serious question.   Mere absence of reasonable determination would only mean that we could
not account for anything, that it was all simply
mysterious and magical.

(vi.) The second question, that of the existence of
disembodied souls, is a mere question of fact.   We
have no ground to suppose that a disembodied condition of the soul would be any gain in spirituality ;
prima facie it might just as well be a loss.   Speaking
generally, we need very much to get a thorough grasp
of the conception that the spiritual is always the
more, and not the less ; to make an abstraction by
cutting off some element of our world is not advan-
cing to what is more spiritual, but is probably retreating
to what is less spiritual.   Of course it is quite true
that a higher totality has extraordinary capacities
for transfiguring and transforming another element
until we may not recognise it again.   This is always
the way in works of art; we can hardly understand
how little details which seem to have no value or
life when seen alone, become so unutterably full of
meaning when we see them in their place.   But

though they seem changed, and are no longer trivial, the principle remains that the spiritual view, or the spiritual being, is always that which has more in it, and never that which has less ; it does not omit, it includes and transforms.   The spiritual view of life, for instance, does not omit the affections, but transforms them ; it takes them up into the whole of life.

To whatever tenuity, then, we may reduce our *matter*, the partial, or narrow, or abstract view of what is best in life, will always be the material and not the spiritual view.   Experience, indeed, rather suggests that what we understand by the spiritual could not exist except by some sort of contrast, such as we have in the *material ;* it always seems to reveal itself through symbols, or in some mode of appearance which rather points to it than actually *is* it, and in the attempt to dispense with the material world there is great risk of turning the spiritual into the material.   This of course is what every spiritualist or ghost-seer does : he finds his spirit creature in a very feeble and attenuated sort of bodily existence.

In completing the science of the realised moral self, what Hegel has called the Science of Objective Mind [1]—mind, that is, as incorporated in law, morality, and the ways of social and political living— we should proceed by taking up from Lecture IX. the conception of a purpose or action having the character of reasonableness.   This character of reasonableness we should analyse and expand, until we had exhibited the moral self as a content at once real and rational, affirmed by the will, which finds in it the true self, or satisfactory life.   But such an

---

[1] See Wallace's translation of Hegel's *Philosophy of Mind;* Dyde's translation of Hegel's *Philosophy of Right.*

investigation, though it would be dealing with the true and essential nature of mind in a far higher degree than inquiries, *e.g.*, as to the relation of body and soul, would go beyond the limits which our definition in Lecture I. assigned to Psychological Science. We should be dealing with the significance of psychical occurrences rather than with their laws and causes. And we therefore end at this point, remembering that our work has only been an introduction to the Science of Mind in the largest and truest sense.

BIBLIOGRAPHY

All students should master Mr. Ward's article in *Encyclopædia Britannica* (Ninth ed. vol. xx.), "Psychology." The number can be obtained separately for 7s. 6d. Mr. Ward's articles in *Mind* (N.S., 5 and 7), and Mr. Bradley's on "Consciousness and Experience" (in *Mind*, N.S., 6), should also be studied, together with the chapter on Association of Ideas in Mr. Bradley's *Principles of Logic.* In lieu of, or in addition to, the above, students may read Mr. Sully's *Human Mind* (2 vols.), Mr. Stout's *Analytic Psychology* (2 vols.), Prof. Wm. James' or Prof. Dewey's *Text-books of Psychology*, or Prof. Höffding's *Outlines of Psychology*. It is strongly urged that the student should, if possible, become possessed of one of these works—by preference that of Mr. Ward—and not merely borrow it from a library. The book should then be thoroughly studied, and any further reading should be undertaken with a view to points which may have proved interesting or difficult in this study. Münsterberg's *Die Willenshandlung* (only 163 pp.) will be found striking and suggestive.

QUESTIONS

1. In what sense is it true that Psychology treats of all that is in the Soul?
2. State and explain Aristotle's definition of " Psyche."
3. What is meant by " atomism " in Psychology?
4. Have we experience of a simple sensation?
5. Criticise the term Association in its psychological usage.
6. What is strictly the meaning of Consciousness?
7. Explain the nature of Apperception.
8. What difficulty is sometimes held to attach to Association by Similarity? Explain by means of an example.
9. What is involved in " Self-assertion "?
10. What are the principal elements in the conception of personal identity?
11. In what principal senses is the term Feeling used by Psychologists?
12. Discuss the view that pleasure and pain can never be objects for consciousness.
13. What is meant by a faculty? Would it be correct to call Attention a faculty?
14. Discuss the view that pleasure is the sole motive of action, explaining how such an idea arises.
15. Illustrate the connection of Will and Intelligence in the developed moral self.
16. Compare the conceptions of " Altruism " and " Self-sacrifice."

17. What is the apparent contradiction in the idea of "reasonable action"?

18. Discuss the connection and relative importance of moral purpose and moral judgment.

19. What views of the relation of body and soul may we venture to set aside as erroneous?

20. In what senses could Free-will be at stake in the problem of Body and Soul?

THE END

Printed by R. & R. Clark, Limited, Edinburgh.